THE SECRET PRAYER

The Three-Step Formula for Attracting Miracles

Copyright © 2015 by Joe Vitale. All rights reserved. Reproduction and distribution are forbidden. No part of this publication shall be reproduced, stored in a retrieval system, or transmitted by any other means, electronic, mechanical, photocopying, recording, or otherwise, without written permission from the author or publisher.

This publication is designed to provide accurate and authoritative information with regard to the subject matter covered. It's sold with the understanding that the author and the publisher are not engaged in rendering legal, intellectual property, accounting, medical, psychological, or other professional advice. If legal advice or other professional assistance is required, the services of a competent professional should be sought. Dr. Joe Vitale and Hypnotic Marketing, Inc. individually or corporately, do not accept any responsibility for any liabilities resulting from the actions of any parties involved.

For more information, please see www.JoeVitale.com or contact Suzanne@mrfire.com.

Or write Hypnotic Marketing, Inc., PO Box 2924, Wimberley, TX 78676.

Cover art and design: Ted Angel
Edited by: Hallagen Ink at www.HallagenInk.com

TABLE OF CONTENTS

Dedication ... v
Foreword ... ix
Acknowledgements ... xiii
Promise Yourself ... xv
Introduction ... xvii

THE FIRST STEP: ACTIVE GRATITUDE

Illumination ... 3
The Divine Whiteboard ... 11
The Mystery of the Secret Prayer ... 15
The Secret of Faith ... 19
Gratitude Makes the World Go Round ... 23
Do It for the Love ... 29
Cleansing Prayers ... 33
Active Gratitude ... 39
Where Do You Pray? ... 43
The Three-Step Formula ... 47
The Hardest Prayer ... 51

THE SECOND STEP: DETACHED REQUEST

How Cool Is That? ... 57
Pray for Angelic Help ... 61
Cowboy Prayers ... 65
Pray and Attract Romance ... 73
The Prayer Wheel ... 77
The Three-Minute Prayer ... 81

In God We Trust	87
A Father's Prayer	93
How to Stop a Hurricane	97
The Prayer Runner	103
Unanswered Prayers	109
The Secret Place of Prayer	113
Scientific Prayer	117
How to Boost Your Prayer Power	121
Prayer without Ceasing	127
Pray It In Writing	133

THE THIRD STEP: INSPIRED ACTION

Pray and Attract Money	139
Pray and See Miracles	145
Pray and Release Weight	149
Pray and Let It Go	153
Prayer is Good Medicine	157
Lincoln's Promise	163
Mind Power Times Two	165
Where Is God?	169
The Gayatri Train	175
The Overlooked Message	179
Peace Talks	183
Afflatus	191
The Ring of Power	197
Pray a Better Future	203
Pray for Others	209
Afterword	211
Prayer Hotlines	215
Bibliography	233
About the Author	237
Follow Dr. Joe Vitale	239
Special Miracles Coaching® Offer!	243

DEDICATION

To Brother Lawrence

There is a place where thou canst touch the eyes
*   Of blinded men to instant, perfect sight;*
There is a place where thou canst say, "Arise"
*   To dying captives, bound in chains of night;*
There is a place where thou canst reach the store
*   Of hoarded gold and free it for the Lord;*
There is a place—upon some distant shore—
Where thou canst send the worker and the Word.
Where is that secret place—dost thou ask, "Where?"
*   O soul, it is the secret place of prayer!*

—Alfred Lord Tennyson

FOREWORD

Most people's prayers sound like letters to Santa Claus.
—Bishop John Shelby Spong

Dear Reader,

Before you begin the journey of transformation that awaits you within these pages, take a moment to consider three questions:

1. HOW DO PEOPLE PRAY?

Human beings are diverse, unique individuals—their lives and mindsets are shaped by distinct circumstances, cultures, and religions. And yet with all of these various influences, prayers around the world tend to be very similar. Most people's prayers are a variation on the theme:

Dear God,
Please give me; give me; give me.
Oh, and give me some more.
Thanks.
Amen.

THE SECRET PRAYER

In other words, most prayers beseech God to give something to the person praying such as improved health, a new job, a better relationship, or a material possession.

Even when our prayers are "for other people," the underlying intent of the request can often be for our own good. For example, "Dear God, please help my brother get a job" may have the hidden meaning "so he'll stop sleeping on my sofa!" Although the prayer is technically for your brother, *you're saying the prayer because it benefits you.*

Throughout the ages, irate ministers have excoriated their flocks for the "sin" of praying for their own self-interest. And, many devout religious people have wrung their hands in sad resignation over the selfishness of "give me" praying.

Perhaps—just perhaps—it is time we consider that the reason so many people pray this way is that *it is natural for us to speak our secret desires to our God trusting that these requests will be heard AND fulfilled.* There exists coded within our very DNA a *knowing* that the way to a better life—a life of health, happiness, love, prosperity, peace, and contentment—is found through asking God to give us what we want.

2. HOW EFFECTIVE IS SUCH PRAYER?

Having been a church minister for more than a decade, I can tell that these *give me* prayers rarely yield the desired

FOREWORD

results. In fact, comedian, philosopher, and societal gadfly George Carlin had it about right when he observed that prayers to God and prayers to the sun yield about the same results: fifty-fifty.

Fifty-fifty—those are pretty lousy odds. If prayer were a vending machine, you'd only get your bottle of water about every *other* time you put money in. You'd go thirsty as often as you'd have a drink. That being the case, you'd probably stop using that particular vending machine.

And yet, we continue to ask. When what we request is not what we receive, we rationalize through a smile of gritted teeth, "Oh, well…it's God's will." Then, we pray for something else—so desperate are we that our benevolent Father, Mother, God, Universe will hear our requests and grant them.

3. WHAT'S THE MISSING SECRET?

If it is natural for us to ask the Divine to bring forth the outcomes, experiences, and possessions we want and begging God isn't working, what's the missing ingredient?

It's *The Secret Prayer*. Rather than just a one-size fits all incantation that attempts to ignite the power of the Universe around you, *The Secret Prayer* is a spiritual shift that ignites the power of the Universe *within* you.

Danish philosopher Søren Kierkegaard hinted at *The Secret Prayer* when he observed, "Prayer does not change

God, but it changes him who prays."

You are about to experience a deep, lasting, and positive shift in all areas of your life.

If you're ready to turn prayer into practical demonstration, then you're ready for *The Secret Prayer*.

Blessings,
Rev. Will Bowen

International best-selling author and founder of *A Complaint Free World (.org)* AND *World Peace 092156 (.org)*

ACKNOWLEDGEMENTS

As with every book I write, numerous people had a helping hand in the process. Mathes Jones created the foundation for this project with her research and initial writing. Suzanne Burns, my right hand assistant for more than ten years now, offered editing and design input. Tanya Brockett of Hallagen Ink offered editorial review. Kent Cummins offered priceless feedback. Ted Angel created the cover art and book layout. Nerissa, my wife, kept me fed and watered throughout the process. I am grateful for all, mentioned or not, who have helped in creating this latest book. May you enjoy it and share it with family and friends. I offer it in love.

PROMISE YOURSELF

To be so strong that nothing can disturb your peace of mind.
To talk health, happiness, and prosperity to every person you meet.
To make all your friends feel that there is something worthwhile in them.
To look at the sunny side of everything and make your optimism come true.
To think only of the best, to work only for the best, and to expect only the best.
To be just as enthusiastic about the success of others as you are about your own.
To forget the mistakes of the past and press on to the greater achievements of the future.
To wear a cheerful expression at all times and give a smile to every living creature you meet.
To give so much time to improving yourself that you have no time to criticize others.
To be too large for worry, too noble for anger, too strong for fear, and too happy to permit the presence of trouble.
To think well of yourself and to proclaim this fact to the world, not in loud word, but in great deeds.
To live in the faith that the whole world is on your side, so long as you are true to the best that is in you.

The original Optimist Creed, written by Christian D. Larson in his 1912 book, *Your Forces and How to Use Them*

INTRODUCTION

Prayer is the effort to bring the human soul into tune with the infinite.

—William James Dawson

From what I can see, prayer has been around since the beginning of time. According to *The Psychology of Prayer*, 97% of all Americans pray at least once a week. Even atheists admit that they sometimes pray.

But as we all know, it doesn't always seem to work. Why not?

What's the secret to having a prayer deliver?

That's what you'll discover in *The Secret Prayer*, where I reveal the three-step formula for attracting miracles through this particular prayer. And I'm talking about anything and everything you could name as a "miracle."

When you think about it, what is impossible?

Since we're talking about enlisting the help of "Something" greater than you, what could be impossible to attract?

Unless you're trying to bend or break the laws of physics, or have an unreal fantasy such as riding a unicorn around the sun, can't you have, do, or be *anything* you can imagine? Aren't the only limits the ones you believe in? Aren't your beliefs open to inspection and change?

I also want to face reality here. Many "new agey" people claim, "It's all good." While everything *is* all good from a *Divine* perspective, from a *physical* perspective, we have work to do.

There are plenty of problems in the world. There are people suffering and starving. You may know some of them. You may be one of them. Dismissing the problems and challenges of life is a form of denial and self-sabotage. You have to be honest and note the issues before us.

And you want to look beyond the issues to Source. When you focus on the peace behind the problem, you begin to clean up the perceptions creating and attracting the problem.

This is why The Secret Prayer is so helpful. It assists you in reconnecting with the essence of life, the Divinity of life, the Source of life. The more you can allow prayer to bring you home, the faster you will nullify the causes of the separation. And then you can see the miracle of right now.

It's worth revealing how I came across The Secret Prayer. You may know me from my books, audios, and movie appearances. You may consider me an inspiration, since I write self-help books, or a huckster, since I sell self-help books. You may like my methods or think they are simply mental diversions from living a life of hard work and struggle.

INTRODUCTION

What you may not know is that I am a seeker like you, and have been since the 1960s, when I was a teenager. Others looked for outside thrills; I looked for inside awakenings. I wanted to know how the world worked, and I wanted to teach it to others. As I discovered new things—such as *Ho'oponopono*—I would share them in books, such as *Zero Limits* and *At Zero*. I simply regarded myself as a scout looking for gold. Whenever I found it, I shared it. I still do that today.

A decade or so ago, I earned one of my doctorates by completing a dissertation on New Thought healers and how they use prayer and "mind treatment" to help people. I found it fascinating but didn't do anything with it.

Then, after the movie *The Secret* made the Law of Attraction mainstream, and made me internationally famous, I wondered how the law blended with prayer. Others wondered, too. People would ask me if I believed in God, or if the Law of Attraction replaced God, and so forth. It made me curious about how we use prayer—if we used it all—to align ourselves with God—or whatever we call The Great Something—to have, do, or be whatever we imagine.

Was that even possible?

As usual, I continued my research and meditating. I was led to rereading the books of Emmet Fox, an author I've always loved. His "mental equivalent" went a long way in helping me realize that everything begins with vivid thought.

THE SECRET PRAYER

Rereading Wallace Wattles's famous book, *Financial Success through Creative Thought*, or, as it is better known by its subtitle, *The Science of Getting Rich*, reminded me that everything comes out of some great energy vortex, and we call it forth with thought and action.

Reading the letters of Brother Lawrence, the beloved monk of the 1600s who taught us to "practice the presence of God," meaning to spend every moment looking for, feeling, and loving the Source, helped me realize the power behind all manifestation was this Divine "Something."

And then one day I had an "aha!" experience.

In some of my books, such as *The Awakening Course*, I explain that we can have peeks into All That Is, and those glimpses are called *satori* experiences in some cultures. I had such an awakening. Somehow the blend of prayer and Law of Attraction merged together into a new formula; a synthesis of ideas that created a powerhouse new system for attracting virtually anything.

I became as excited as if I had been hit by lightning or the heavens opened and some Great Being had spoken to me directly. This new prayer was powerful. It *is* powerful. I put up an audio of me leading people through The Secret Prayer on www.TheSecretPrayer.com. Instantly, thousands of people went to it, used it, and began to rave about it.

Will it work for you, too?

Yes.

INTRODUCTION

How can I say that?

When you realize that you are *already* a manifester and are *already* living a miracle for which you are grateful (the first step in the formula), then you can stop there. You *already* attracted something incredible. But add the next two steps—detached request and inspired action—and your further results are virtually guaranteed.

I'm calling it a "secret" prayer because your prayer should be between you and your inner connection to "All That Is." I've learned that sharing your prayers with others could weaken their power. Rather than invite doubt or negativity, keep your prayer to yourself. Let it be a "secret" between you and Divinity.

We'll explore all of this together in this book. To get you started, here's the crash course in The Secret Prayer:

1. Active Gratitude
2. Detached Request
3. Inspired Action

If you only read this far and, in your future prayers, approach them from this perspective, you won't be disappointed. Of course, I hope you'll continue reading because I'll explore each of these in more depth, as well as offer other fascinating tidbits to satisfy your curiosity about prayer.

It's been my experience that most people don't actually believe their prayers. They pray without any real belief that anyone is listening or anything will happen. They simply "toss" one to the sky, like a stranded person on an island throwing a note in a bottle into the ocean. They hope someone picks it up. Then they hope someone acts on their plea.

Desperation is another problem. Most prayers are just begging. People pray for help, solutions, miracles, healing, money, and more. But when they pray, it's often because they don't see a way out and plead for intervention.

Even when they do get an answer or an inspiration, most people don't take action. This is common in the world of metaphysics. People often think praying is the only action they need to take. It may be *an* action, but it's not the entire blueprint to results. Prayer is a way to activate the Law of Attraction by requesting an intention and inviting inspiration.

As I've written and talked about in many places, it's not always easy to distinguish where an idea is coming from. Is it the voice of the Divine? Or the ever-wily ego?

But not this time.

When I heard the call to write about this, I knew immediately it was from the Divine. I could *feel* it. And immediately, I set out to work. I knew I wanted this to be not only inspirational, but also fresh, interesting, fun, and insightful, playful even. As I began, I received more guidance and inspiration about how to do this—which books to read, stories to tell, and people to reference, both old and new. This book is the result of that inquiry.

INTRODUCTION

What you are holding is the answer to my own secret prayer.

I pray it will help you with yours.

Expect Miracles.

Love,
Dr. Joe Vitale
Austin, Texas
www.MrFire.com
May 2015
PS—I love you.

THE FIRST STEP: ACTIVE GRATITUDE

A joke…

Once you enter the prayer loop, it's pretty difficult to get out. You pray. Usually for something to be thankful for. You either receive it or you don't. If you do, you pray and give thanks. If you don't, you pray and ask *again* for something to be thankful for. Genuflect and repeat until death.

ILLUMINATION

But in truth our very ideas about logic and how one ought to come to conclusions about the nature of reality are informed by the usually unacknowledged presuppositions of the world in which we live. So the first step in trying to think about miracles is to see the presuppositions we bring to our thinking.
—Eric Metaxas, *Miracles*

In mid-2014, I e-mailed a survey to my subscribers. I wanted to know which title of a weight loss book would interest them. I had transformed my body and wanted to share my insights and processes in a book. But I didn't know what to call it. I included several titles about health, fitness, weight loss, and longevity. Out of sheer inspiration, I added a couple titles that simply came to mind: one about visualization and the other about prayer.

They were throwaway titles, inserted so people wouldn't think I was stacking the deck in the survey so they would only vote for a weight loss book. Even though that was exactly what I was doing, to my surprise, few wanted a book on health and fitness from me. Instead, the overwhelming majority wanted a book about prayer.

I hadn't thought about prayer much. I prayed every day,

and still do. I've been doing it for years. But I didn't plan to write an entire book about it. To test myself, I wrote an article about a three-step formula for getting results through prayer. The three steps came from meditation. They felt inspired. The article gave an overview of them. I posted it on my blog. Then I sent an e-mail to my list, inviting them to go read it. They did. And they loved it.

It was clear that I needed to write a book about prayer.

I started thinking about it and decided to call it *The Secret Prayer*. As I mentioned in the Introduction, it is "secret" because the prayer is between you and your creator. I tied it to the Law of Attraction, and my being in the movie *The Secret*, with the title and subtitle: *The three-step formula for attracting miracles*.

But I didn't feel ready to write an actual book yet. So I hired a ghostwriter to begin the process. I told her to write short chapters about praying and prayer. I let her generate her own ideas. As she did that, I did my own thinking and research. I started rereading old books about prayer, and new ones. I was overwhelmed by the amount of books published on the subject. Nobody seemed to have one way to pray. Nobody had a guaranteed way to pray. I found all of it curious, but lacking.

Meanwhile, my ghostwriter turned in some chapters. They were beautifully written, and interesting, but didn't reveal any great secret. I wanted to go deeper. I wanted to uncover what truths lay behind prayer. I thanked my ghostwriter for her services, and embarked on my own,

ILLUMINATION

deeper journey.

As I thought about prayer, I was led to such interesting books as a rare biography of Emmet Fox by Harry Gaze. Fox was the New Thought teacher who wrote many bestselling books, including an important booklet called *The Mental Equivalent*. I found Fox fascinating. He seemed sincere and focused and was articulate in explaining that prayer was for us to get right with God, not for God to get right with us.

The biography also talked about someone called Brother Lawrence, and his message of "Practicing the Presence of God." I had never heard of Brother Lawrence. But apparently his practice deeply influenced Fox. So I dug deeper.

It turns out that Brother Lawrence was a monk in Paris in the 1600s who had an awakening at the age of eighteen. He was looking at a leaf (some stories say he was looking at a barren tree) and suddenly saw how it contained the past, the future, death, life, and all else. It triggered an experience of realizing God was in all. From that point on, he lived his life, until his passing at age eighty, doing his best to stay conscious of the "presence" of God in every moment. His teachings, available in a little booklet compiled after his death and titled, *The Practice of the Presence of God*, still influence people today.

Including me.

I read Brother Lawrence's words and somehow

awakened to the reality of the Divine in and around us. Life took on a glow; a kind of luminosity; an illumination. I would look out through the same eyes but everything I saw had brightness to it, as if it were somehow more animated and empowered with even more life. It made me smile. It made me feel love and loved.

As I write these words, that illumination is right here. I notice that as long as I remind myself of the "presence of God" all around me, the luminosity remains. As soon as my mind drifts into worry or doubt or gets caught up in the day's activities, the light dims.

In those off moments, I could bring the wattage back up by reminding myself of Brother Thomas and Emmet Fox. They urged us to stop and meditate on the presence in the moment. That helped. And if I needed more help, I would practice the Hawaiian Ho'oponopono healing prayer: *I love you, I'm sorry, please forgive me, thank you.* I would simply repeat those phrases as a type of cleansing prayer.

As I did this, I realized that all of life was a big theatrical show. The world I saw and lived was a movie. The people in it, characters. The drama of life was the story line and plot. Behind it all, running the show, is this God/Divine/Nature/The Great Something. And the show was being put on for It to educate and entertain itself, through me, and of course, through you.

Whenever my mind seemed to wander or wonder, I'd remind myself that the show was going on and I was a character in it. Anything that kept me from seeing the beauty of now was simply data/beliefs/programming limiting my view. The more I could be here now and enjoy the flow, and the show, the more life was a miracle.

When I looked at others, I saw the invisible programming that caused them to behave as they did. Their personalities were nests of beliefs. They became interesting characters, wired to say and do what I saw. I realized that they looked at their lives through mental filters. Most considered themselves victims. Few knew that the victim mentality stemmed from victim programming. They were living out their beliefs. Their outer lives were a projection of their inner world. As Emmet Fox wrote in *Sparks of Truth*, "Whatever you experience in your life is really but the outpicturing of your own thoughts and beliefs." But few know that as a firsthand reality.

I realized that if I just saw through the costume and the role, I could see the light inside each person. I could see the Divine within, probably like Brother Lawrence saw the whole and holy world unfold by looking at a leaf or a barren tree.

During this time, returning from a trip to see my family, I wandered into an airport bookstore. There in front of me was a book titled, *Miracles*. I smiled, not being surprised at all. When you are in the flow, you are in the know. Little "coincidences" happen that aren't orchestrated by you or me at all. The Great Something

THE SECRET PRAYER

nudges everyone to help everyone further along his or her path. I was nudged into a bookstore to see a book. It was a sign. It makes sense: the Greek word for miracle is "simaios," which means, "sign."

Reading *Miracles* on the flight, I came across this line: *"Even though prayers are not offered only to get a desired result, there is little doubt that most miracles are the result of prayer."*

The implication is that we have to trust as we pray. We realize it's all Divine, and we make our requests for what *we think* is good for us. But we can't pretend to *really* know what is good for us. If there is intelligence behind it all, call it what you may, It has access to all possibilities that we can't possibly see from our little views of the world. And It has a bigger and better plan for us.

So we gratefully practice the presence of the Divine (the first step), ask for what we want (the second step), and still allow the presence to run the show *through* us (the third step).

When we are prompted to act (what I call Inspired Action—the third step), we act. That, too, is the Divine living through us. It is the Divine giving us a cue that we are wanted on stage. And death, by extension, is the Divine calling us *off* stage. Our current part is done. We bow and exit. The play continues.

I now feel the "presence of Divinity" in each moment, and that may be the greatest secret prayer of them all.

Best of all, you can do this too.

ILLUMINATION

Feel God.
Allow God.
Express God.

If you practice this as your first and only step, you will be living the miracle. Everything after that is a gift; a continuation of the miracle.

Look around.

See if you can spot "the presence" right now.

This moment is the miracle.

You are the miracle.

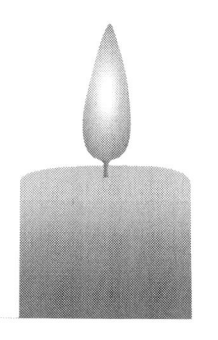

THE DIVINE WHITEBOARD

Supply yourself with a mental equivalent, and the thing must come to you.

—Emmet Fox

Since around 2005, I've been using the term "Whiteboard" to refer to the higher power that fills our lives with life. The reason I use *Whiteboard* is because so many people have baggage around the terms God, or Universe, that they can't hear or see the great gift that awaits them. They are too busy judging it to use it.

When I talk about the Whiteboard of life, I am referring to the background "witness" behind all your thoughts, feelings, and behaviors. I want you to understand this, so please follow along in this short meditation:

You have thoughts, but you are not your thoughts. You can observe them, so you are somehow detached from them. What is it in you that observes your own thoughts?

You have feelings but you are not your own feelings. You can notice when you are upset or happy, so you are somehow not those feelings. If you are separate from your feelings, who are you that is observing them?

THE SECRET PRAYER

You have a body but you are not your body. You can feel it and observe it and report on it and use it, but you are somehow not it. If you are using your body, who is the "you" that is using it?

In other words, if you aren't your thoughts, or your feelings, or your body, then who is the observer or witness to it all?

That background witness is what I am calling the Whiteboard. It is like the sky, and clouds are thoughts that float by on it. It is like a sheet of artist paper, and what you draw on it is like the feelings you experience and watch change.

The Whiteboard is the source of life. You can send requests into it—through The Secret Prayer—and you can receive inspiration from it—also through The Secret Prayer.

When you relax to implement The Secret Prayer, it's useful to keep in mind the image of the Whiteboard. You can imagine giving thanks to the power source of life, and you can imagine writing requests on the Whiteboard. You can also imagine that the Whiteboard sends you images as inspirations.

The Whiteboard is simply a neutral image to help you use The Secret Prayer with greater impact. It isn't to replace God or any word that you use to represent that ultimate loving force. It's just an option; another tool to help you focus on thanking, requesting, and listening.

This is fundamentally important because all the

THE DIVINE WHITEBOARD

healers I have studied have one thing in common: they look *past* the problem or request to the witness behind it. The healers may hear your plea for a healing or your request for a manifestation, but they look *behind* it to what I call the Whiteboard.

Said another way, many "new agey" people claim, "It's all good." While everything *is* all good from a Divine perspective, from a *physical* perspective, we have work to do. There are plenty of problems in the world. There are people suffering and starving. You may know some of them. You may be one of them. Dismissing the problems and challenges of life is a form of denial and self-sabotage. You have to be honest and note the issues before us.

And you want to look beyond the issues to Source. Again, I call this background underneath it all the Whiteboard. When you focus on the peace behind the problem, you begin to clean up the perceptions creating and attracting the problem.

This is why prayer is so helpful. It assists you in reconnecting with the essence of life, the Divinity of life, the Source of life. The more you can allow prayer to bring you home, the faster you will nullify the causes of the separation. The more you identify with the Whiteboard—which you are welcome to call God, Nature, Energy, Universe, or any other word you prefer—the more you can begin to see, feel, and experience the miracle of right now.

Let me give you one more way to look at this: I created

THE SECRET PRAYER

a self-help method called The Secret Mirror to help you look past your problems. The idea is to look in a mirror but look *within* the image. You will see yourself of course, at first. But as you gaze into your own eyes, you can begin to see the *essence* of you. This essence is what you want to focus on to have, do, or be what you imagine. This essence within you is the Whiteboard.

Another way to look at this essence within is to consider the word *Pneuma*. This is the ancient Greek word for spirit or soul or the God inside. I was reminded of the word while reading Emmet Fox's little known book, *The Science of Living*. Fox said it is our Divine self.

All of these words are to help you get past the baggage of definitions and to the real you—the essence behind it all—the Divine you.

THE MYSTERY OF THE SECRET PRAYER

The secret is to go with the mystery.
—Judith Orloff, M.D.

I went to a movie the other day, *Magic in the Moonlight*, a film by Woody Allen set in the 1920s starring Colin Firth and Emma Stone. It came recommended to me by a friend; although she didn't tell me anything about it other than that I might enjoy it.

As it turned out, it was quite different than I had imagined—not so much in story but in its impact on me.

Here's why: *How could it know I was writing a book on prayer?*

It's a crazy question, right? But that's the thing that struck me when, towards the end of the movie, Colin Firth's character, an abrupt, egotistical atheist who worships the school of cold logic, began praying and discussing the "power of prayer."

Suddenly this romantic comedy took on a whole new level of conversation and meaning. I sat spellbound, riveted to my chair.

Now, obviously, it didn't "know" I was writing a book about this subject. But *something* did…something within me. And that something took me to see that particular film at that particular time to hear a particular conversation onscreen.

This phenomenon is what's known as *synchronicity*, which the Oxford dictionary describes as "the simultaneous occurrence of events that appear significantly related but have no discernible causal connection."

In other words, romantic comedy + prayer soliloquy + moviegoer writing a book on prayer = synchronicity.

According to Judith Orloff, M.D., author of *Second Sight*, "Synchronicity is a sign that we are intuitively attuned, not only to our immediate friends and family, but also to the greater collective."

It is, she says, "…a state of grace," and I agree.

In that moment, I knew I was on the right course in writing this book. The idea had come to me in what felt like divine inspiration, and this confirmed it.

It was, indeed, a *sign*.

I have written much about this state of grace as it relates to you and your relationship with the Divine, with what I sometimes call Zero. To me, it places you squarely in the realm of magic and miracles.

It's a powerful place to be.

Now here's the million-dollar question: *How do you get there?*

How do you access your own unique connection to something that exists within you, a source—whether you call it the Divine, God, Spirit, the Universe, or something else—which offers every answer to every problem and every desire you could possibly seek?

The answer is what I call The Secret Prayer.

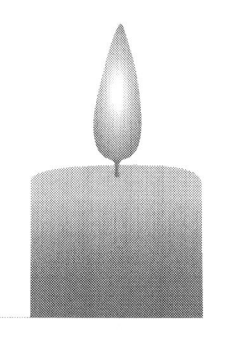

THE SECRET OF FAITH

Whatever you experience in your life is really but the outpicturing of your own thoughts and beliefs.
—Emmet Fox

Who or what is running the planet, anyway?

Every culture, every religion, and every philosophy has a theory. And there are even groups who believe nothing operates the planet and we're all just an accident of nature.

What's correct?

After all, if you or I pray, who or what are we praying *to?*

Back in 1927, an advertising man and best-selling author wrote this passage in his book, *What Can a Man Believe?*:

Faith in business, faith in the country, faith in one's self, faith in other people—this is the power that moves the world. And why is it unreasonable to believe that this power, which is so much stronger than any other, is merely a fragment of the Great Power, which operates the universe?

Barton didn't need to name "The Great Power" for you and I to reach an agreement that there is *something* behind it all. Various religions and philosophies place names on this "something," but we are all pointing to the same thing. Even atheists, when they say there is nothing but nature operating the world, are actually calling the "Great Something" by the name *Nature*.

In short, we can all agree that there is some sort of mysterious power behind all we see. It may be invisible, but it can be felt. And while it may not be visible to the naked eye, it has intelligence and it is giving us life.

This is why the first step in the Secret Prayer is so important. Active Gratitude is about realizing that we are given life. We didn't ask for it or pay for it. We were *given* it.

And life itself—the "Great Something"—is supporting us by regulating the planet, giving us oxygen and sunshine, and keeping us from floating into space with gravity, and more. Even our bodies are being regulated with blood flow and nervous system activity, while we didn't request it or pay for it. We were *given* that, too.

Even if you argue about how or why life is sustaining you, and who or what is behind it all, you'd have to admit that a whole lot is going on that you consciously have nothing to do with. It has been given to you.

Active Gratitude is the single most important step in the formula because it's all you need to attract more good into your life. If you really and truly came from an inner attitude of genuine gratitude for your life—even for the current struggles in it—you'd begin to attract more good to be more grateful for.

Please don't dismiss this as wishy-washy or airy-fairy or woo-woo. The idea of what you focus on expanding goes back to William James, the great psychologist. He said, "The greatest revolution of our generation is the discovery that human beings, by changing the inner attitudes of their minds, can change the outer aspects of their lives."

The "Great Something" has already given you life. Be grateful for that, and more good will come your way—automatically, easily, effortlessly, and naturally.

GRATITUDE MAKES THE WORLD GO ROUND

If the only prayer you say in your life is 'thank you,' that would suffice.

—Meister Eckhart

I have a nightly ritual.

I call it my gratitude hour.

During this time, I sit in my hot tub outside under the Texas stars, and I thank the Divine for everything and anything going on in my life. Even the not-so-good stuff. Sometimes I'll talk to the stars and whisper a Hawaiian Ho'oponopono prayer, which are these four simple phrases:

I love you. I'm sorry. Please forgive me. Thank you.

One of the purposes of this hour is to create a space to receive, which I initiate through gratitude. It's the secret to attracting anything you want. That's why it's step one in The Secret Prayer formula.

How does it do this?

For one thing, you cannot find gratitude in your heart and not be changed, physically. It's the single most powerful thing you can do to transform yourself in any moment, no matter where you are. It clears and cleans everything unlike itself. If you have a problem, saying thank you is a way to acknowledge the Divine for taking care of it. It is the gateway to forgiveness of self and others because we are all divinely connected.

Gratitude is the great scourer of the mind.

But it does more…

It is the pathway to miracles.

When you move into an active state of sincere gratitude, your whole being lights up and your energy quickens, and this high vibration acts like a magnet to bring your good to you. If I were to suggest how this happens, it would be that when you're in gratitude, you naturally want to give—praise, love, even material things. As you give, you create a vacuum or space for the Divine to fill. Gratitude, giving, and receiving go hand-in-hand.

It also has the power to anchor or center you in the present moment, where all your good is to be found. In my Miracles Coaching® calls, we begin with a gratitude prayer and meditation. It's a powerful method in the group for connecting everyone. You do this by choosing something in your immediate world or surroundings to focus on in gratitude. Here's an example from one of the calls that a Miracles Coach offered that evening:

Tonight I'm feeling especially grateful for my wife. I've had the privilege of caring for her today as she's been ill, and helping out with my children. Without my wife, I would be less than the individual that I am. I'm grateful for her smile. I'm grateful for her radiance and her patience. I'm grateful for her personality, her love, and her compassion. I'm grateful for her belief and her support.

I'm grateful for moments of silence, moments of conversation, and moments of laughter. I'm grateful for the way she looks at me when she wants to give me the signal that I'm out of line, and the way she looks at me when she wants me to know that she's absolutely madly and deeply in love with me. I'm grateful for the way she nurtures our children, the way she educates them, and the way she is the glue for our entire family. I'm grateful for my wonderful wife.

Can you imagine how this person's wife feels because of this person's gratitude? She doesn't have to be in the room or even hear it, although it's good to express your gratitude to the ones you love. Whether you do or not, they feel it through the divine connection we all share.

At the same time, you don't have to look for the obvious thing to be grateful for. It can be anything, even the most seemingly insignificant thing. It's amazing what joy and service the smallest object brings to our lives and to everyone who shared in creating it, as you can see from this next gratitude prayer. This Miracles Coach chose a small pottery bowl:

Thank you, bowl, for being in my life and for being

present in this corner of my desk to brighten and beautify this corner of my life. I am so deeply appreciative of your rich red, which reminds me of manifestation and the root chakra. I appreciate your red color, beautiful little pottery bowl.

Thank you for reminding me how connected to the earth we are as I think about the clay, which the potter utilized to mold and shape you, beautiful pottery bowl.

Thank you for holding these healing gemstones and rocks that resonate with vibration, which I so appreciate, enjoy, and feel. I am very appreciative that you are here in my life, little pottery bowl.

Thank you to the potter. Thank you for adding your energy to this bowl so that I can have this pottery bowl beautifying the corner of my desk. I appreciate you for crafting this with love and for bringing that love into my life every day as I look at this beautiful pottery bowl. Thank you. Thank you for this moment and how I feel my vibration rise to that of gratitude as I hold you in my awareness.

Thank you. Thank you. Thank you.

Doesn't just reading these gratitude prayers make your heart sing? That is the vibrational lift of gratitude.

As you explore and deepen your own gratitude for all that is in your life, you will feel your whole body, mind, outlook, perspective, and paradigm change. That moment becomes an inspired moment, one you're fully present in.

GRATITUDE MAKES THE WORLD GO ROUND

This is the stage you set for step two in The Secret Prayer formula—Detached Request. Out of this state of being, your next moments will then be even more beautiful, and you'll begin to attract more things, more experiences, and more moments to be grateful for.

Gratitude answers everything.

DO IT FOR THE LOVE

Prayer is a soul's sincere desire, uttered or unexpressed.
—Old hymn

After reading an ABC7News article that tattoos are on the rise among professionals, I decided to do a quick Google search to find out why people are willing to endure the hours of pain to get them. There were all the usual suspects: for personal identity, to honor loved ones, even for profit (advertising space can be pricey).

But to pray?

Yes, that, too, apparently, with the majority of artwork in this genre appearing to be the well-known *Serenity Prayer* or an image of praying hands. No surprises there—they're both fairly common. Not to diminish them, I doubt there's a gift store in Texas that doesn't have either framed pictures or coffee mugs emblazoned with one or the other.

Then I stumbled upon Michael Franti.

At a towering six feet six inches, he's the lead singer for the band Spearhead, whose music is known for its positive messaging. A highly conscious musician, he's also an activist with his own foundation: Do It for the

THE SECRET PRAYER

Love.

I became really excited when I discovered he has not one, but two, prayer tattoos. Reading the inspiration behind them, I couldn't help being completely enchanted and my guess is that you'll be, too.

On his left arm are the words, "Today I pray for _____." The blank line is included, and each day either he, or his partner Sara, fills it in with a Sharpie. Sometimes he's praying for someone or something in particular, which he's very specific about—"my mom" or "rain" or a "friend." Or, if he's playing a concert, he might even let a fan write in whatever they want to pray for.

"It's about positivity," he says. "There're a lot of people who come to our shows who aren't feeling positive or openhearted, and they want to get that experience from the music that night that we're playing in their town. I think [having them fill in the tattoo] is another way to help someone feel positive about whatever situation they're in."

If that's not inspiring enough, he also has an image of a bird that turns into a fish then into a prayer, depicted by an arrow, on both forearms running from his elbows to his little finger. He calls it a "prayer of abundance" that originates from a story in Tahiti.

In Tahiti, the birds live up in the trees, and in the morning they go out into the water. The fishermen watch from the shore and see where the birds are diving into

DO IT FOR THE LOVE

the water to get fish, which angle they're going in, how long they stay in the water... and then from all that, the fishermen are able to tell which direction to approach in their boats to not scare the fish, and how deep to cast their nets. So if you watch the signs in your life, you will get what you need—you'll get your bounty. Be observant and be still at times.

I love this prayer and story. It not only clearly explains the basis of receiving your sustenance and nourishment on a daily basis; it shows how uniquely different cultures see the truth of things in the world around them. Even if you're not a fisherman, you can appreciate the analogy and its message of practicing mindfulness.

In other words, it isn't a question of the Divine providing—it's a question of how well you can be still and pay attention.

These are the roots that form your secret prayer.

CLEANSING PRAYERS

Most human relations problems would melt away if the people involved would pray prayers of release, instead of trying to make people over to conform to their will and their way.

—Catherine Ponder

A number of years ago I read an incredible story about unconditional love by a dear friend of mine, Barry Neil Kaufman, affectionately known as "Bears." Besides being a best-selling author, he and his wife, Samahria, are the co-founders of the world renowned Option Institute International Learning & Training Center, where they offer personal growth programs using their Option Process®.

In the article, he shared an experience he had with a mother and her young daughter who had come to the institute for help. Apparently, from the time this child was born, she'd had anorexia (an eating disorder), and had been passed from one doctor to another in an effort to get her to eat. Finally, they had resorted to force-feeding.

Barry explained to the mother that at the institute their methodology was to honor the child's will, which meant the mother would have to let go completely and let her daughter decide. Was she willing to do this no matter what could happen? At first, she said she couldn't do it; what if her daughter died? The mother tussled with this for weeks until one day she came to see Barry and told him that she was finally at peace about everything. She could accept her daughter unconditionally.

Unbeknownst to them, at that exact moment, *her daughter took her first bite of food in a room across campus.*

How could this happen?

This is the power of release—and the secret behind cleansing prayers.

In her book, *The Dynamic Laws of Prayer*, Catherine Ponder says that your unanswered prayers are often due to unresolved and hostile feelings you are harboring or "possessiveness" towards another person. It's emotional energy that is channeled inappropriately and away from your own life. In order to release them, you say a cleansing prayer of some kind.

In my book, *At Zero*, I talk about Morrnah Simeona who created the modern-day version of Ho'oponopono. Morrnah believed that *aka chords* bind us to people and that only as we are able to cut those emotional ties can the Divine truly operate freely through us. She had a favorite prayer for doing this.

Cleansing Prayer
Spirit, Superconscious, please locate the origin of my feelings,

CLEANSING PRAYERS

thoughts of (_____fill in the blank with your belief, feeling, or thought_____).
Take each and every level, layer, area, and aspect of my being to this origin.
Analyze it and resolve it perfectly with God's truth.
Come through all generations of time and eternity, healing every incident and its appendages based on the origin.
Please do it according to God's will until I am at the present, filled with light and truth, God's peace and love, forgiveness of myself for my incorrect perceptions, and forgiveness of every person, place, circumstances, and events, which contributed to this—these feelings and thoughts.

She used this prayer in many situations, even to release someone's spirit once they had passed on. In each case, she would repeat the prayer four times.

You can use cleansing prayers for anything—business, marriage, friendship, health, wealth—wherever it's needed to restore harmony in you. For example, if you have a quarrelsome relationship in any matter, you could say something like, "I fully and freely release you. I know that the Divine is working in and through you and I let go completely now. You are free and I am free, too."

It isn't always because of negative people or someone else that you might want to use a cleansing prayer. It could be that you need to release the past as you're holding on to it. Maybe you need to forgive yourself for something you did or did not do. Or perhaps you need to release a

THE SECRET PRAYER

belief or a need you had. I remember hearing Louise Hay once suggest saying something like, "I release the need to be [fill in the blank]." For example:

I release the need to be disappointed.
I release the need to be unsafe.
I release the need to be angry.
I release the need to be in poverty.
I release the need to be alone.

Aristotle said, "Nature abhors a vacuum," and this is the basis for using a cleansing prayer. Anytime you let something go, emotionally or physically, internally or externally, you are cleansing yourself and your life, and thus creating a vacuum or space for something better to enter.

For my book, *At Zero*, I wrote a cleansing prayer to help me through the process of writing. I also included it in the front matter of the book to continue its cleansing work:

Oh, Infinite Divine Mind,
Through my beloved High Self,
Cleanse this unit of all negativity,
Both within and without,
That it may be a perfect vessel for
Your Presence.

CLEANSING PRAYERS

Another very simple, elegant and effective way to cleanse any form of negativity within you is through repeating the four phrases of Ho'oponopono, which is the method Dr. Hew Len used to heal an entire ward of criminally insane people, which I wrote about in my book, *Zero Limits*. These four phrases are:

I'm sorry.
Please forgive me.
Thank you.
I love you.

When you say these words over and over, in essence it's a mantra running in the background of any activity you're doing, whether it's having a conversation with someone, baking a pie, building a company, or anything else. You're continually releasing on your thoughts and judgments in order to allow the Divine to work through you on behalf of yourself and others for the highest good. When used this way, it's a kind of shorthand, much like poetry could be considered shorthand for literature.

On the other hand, you could say there is a literary or extended version of the four phrases. For example, if you have a specific situation you want to address, like an argument with your partner, you might say something like:

I'm sorry. I have no idea what program was in me that caused

THE SECRET PRAYER

the argument with my partner, but please forgive me for being unconscious of my own thought pattern. Thank you for taking care of this, and I love you."

In this prayer, I'm speaking directly to God, to the Divine. What I love about the simplicity of this is that you're covering all the bases of the three-step formula here:

1. **Active Gratitude**—Thanking the Divine.
2. **Detached Request**—The intention is implied—you wouldn't be saying this prayer if you didn't have an intention of harmony with your partner.
3. **Inspired Action**—Allowing the Divine to take care of this through you and others.

In the same way a cleansing prayer creates a vacuum in the universe, what you will discover is that it opens a space in your own mind, which then can be filled with a sense of relief, relaxation, and peace. It redirects your energies away from the problem and frees them to go where you would rather direct them.

Whether you need to dissolve, resolve, or take a next step, cleansing prayers can eliminate any roadblocks to your good.

ACTIVE GRATITUDE

We live in a belief driven universe. Change your beliefs and you get a different universe.

—Dr. Joe Vitale

Every month I answer questions from people in my Miracles Coaching® program. I have been doing it for years. The questions are always raw, in depth, fresh, sincere, and often surprising. For example:
- How do I stay positive when people around me are negative?
- How do I discover my life purpose when I don't know what I want?
- How do I attract money in this terrible economy?
- How do I attract my soul mate?
- How do I improve my self-image?
- How do I help others?
- What can I do when everything looks hopeless?

Every call is recorded, and the best of the questions and answers get put into a series of books called, *The Miracles Manual*. There are currently two volumes in the series with a third on the way.

Recently, I had this question tossed at me:

THE SECRET PRAYER

"If you were forced to set all learning aside and could only teach one principle for the rest of your life, what one principle would hold the most importance to you?"

"I can answer that question in just two words," I replied.

"Oh?"

"Active Gratitude."

"Active Gratitude?"

I went on to say, "If each of us would practice gratitude in the moment, all worries would vanish, all problems would resolve, all miracles would come easily—in fact, if we *really* were in gratitude in the moment, we'd realize we are *already* happy, *already* peaceful, and *already* living the miracle."

Active Gratitude means *noticing the good in every moment*. When you actually come from gratitude, you wouldn't judge the moment as good or bad because you'd realize the jury isn't in yet; so *every* moment can be seen *as good*.

Active Gratitude means you live in a spirit of thankfulness, realizing all you have right now is a gift and a miracle in itself.

Active Gratitude means your meditation is gratitude, your process is gratitude, your prayer is gratitude, and your technique is gratitude.

Active Gratitude means giving thanks in each moment *for* the moment.

If each of us practiced Active Gratitude, we would

ACTIVE GRATITUDE

change ourselves and the planet, and would probably invite instant enlightenment.

In each moment, the Universe is giving us so much that we rarely acknowledge—It is keeping us alive without our paying or doing *a thing*. If we realized this with Active Gratitude, we would feel overwhelmed with love.

Active Gratitude would open our eyes to see the miracle of right now.

And from practicing Active Gratitude, we would have raised our vibration so all we attract in the future moments would be better and better, always raising the bar on the incredible beauty of the now.

There's a reason gratitude is the first step in The Secret Prayer formula: it's an acknowledgement of all you have *already* been given, which in turns creates a type of magnetic field that attracts more to be grateful for.

Why don't we practice Active Gratitude?

We are afraid.

We subconsciously think some version of this belief: "If I'm happy and accept this moment as good, I won't do anything to make my life better."

But is that true?

I've discovered that when I am happy, content, and at peace, I tend to pursue my calling, my life path, and my life mission.

When I lived in fear, desperation, and survival, all I attracted was more of the same.

THE SECRET PRAYER

The secret door to escape the mental torment of suffering is to begin the practice of praising.

In other words, look around and find what you are thankful for, and express it.

Yes, if I was backed into a corner and told I could only teach one thing, it would be Active Gratitude.

And I'd be grateful for that, too.

Any more questions?

WHERE DO YOU PRAY?

"Hello, God. How are you? I'm Liz. It's nice to meet you." That's right—I was speaking to the creator of the universe as though we'd just been introduced at a cocktail party. But we work with what we know in this life, and these are the words I always use at the beginning of a relationship.
—Elizabeth Gilbert, *Eat Pray Love*

Elizabeth Gilbert was on the bathroom floor when she uttered the words above. Considering that book was an international bestseller, I guess it goes to show you can pray just about anywhere. But not all relationships are like that. Whether you're kneeling in the bathroom, a church or synagogue, by your bed, at the table, or not kneeling at all, the Divine gets it.

I thought that was pretty much the end of that discussion, until I found out about "thin places." It sounds like something out of a science fiction novel, doesn't it? The moment I heard the words, I felt a tug on my curiosity, which I discovered was for good reason: There may be "better" places to pray than others. Thinner places, anyway.

According to my research, a thin place is an actual

physical place on earth where the separation between this world and the eternal or "other world" seems to "collapse." In a *New York Times* article, author Eric Weiner says that "the ancient pagan Celts, and later, Christians, used the term to describe mesmerizing places like the wind-swept isle of Iona or the rocky peaks of Croagh Patrick. Heaven and earth, the Celtic saying goes, are only three feet apart, but in thin places that distance is even shorter."

A thin place may be considered sacred or not, as Weiner describes above, or it could be an ancient mosque or ruins. A friend of mine told me that when she was a young girl growing up in Turkey, she and her family would often visit a place called "Heaven and Hell," a site of the early Christians. Here, two craters sit side-by-side in the ground; one of them was used to pitch people over the cliff into a seemingly bottomless abyss (Hell), and the other had a narrow, steep switchback trail accessible only by foot which led to a small church hidden down below (Heaven).

The most notable thing about a thin place is the way you *feel* when you're there. It's a palpable sense of the mysterious, of the presence or power of the Divine, or, as Weiner calls it, the "Infinite Whatever."

Mindie Burgoyne, who writes about and leads tours to thin places, describes them this way: "Thin places captivate our imagination, yet diminish our existence. We become very small, yet we gain connection and become part of something larger than we can perceive."

WHERE DO YOU PRAY?

For some people, the notion of thin places can extend to a place in your mind—those states of being that allow you to experience the Divine intimately. Others, like Burgoyne, take offense to that, insisting that thin places are always and only real, earthly designations. She says, "thin places should not be confused with thin moments, those being times when that mysterious power is felt during a particular experience or synchronistic course of events...."

One thing that's agreed upon is that, however you experience a thin place, whether you travel with your feet or your mind, they offer a glimpse or viewpoint beyond the mundane details of everyday life. Weiner says, "In thin places, we become our more essential selves."

As physical places, thin places aren't necessarily ancient or historical in nature. It seems they can be everywhere—even bookstores, which I was glad to know. But, apparently you can be in one and not be aware of it depending on your level of spiritual openness. Perhaps you have to be attuned in some way to the Divine. How much, who knows? I like how Weiner puts it.

If God (however defined) is everywhere and "everywhen," as the Australian aboriginals put it so wonderfully, then why are some places thin and others not? Why isn't the whole world thin? Maybe it is but we're too thick to recognize it. Maybe thin places offer glimpses not of heaven but of earth as it really is, unencumbered. Unmasked.

THE SECRET PRAYER

The good thing about prayer is it's portable, so if you do find yourself in a thin place, it would be an excellent time to pray, to commune with the Divine. It probably won't get any better. On the other hand, maybe, like Elizabeth Gilbert, your bathroom floor is just fine. Like Confucius said, "…no matter where you go, there you are." And it just might be a thin place.

THE THREE-STEP FORMULA

When you put yourself into the state of the wish fulfilled, and think from it, you are praying, and in a way your reasoning mind does not know, your wish will become a fact in your world. You can be the man or woman you want to be, when you know how to pray.

—Neville Goddard

Who knew there was a right way to pray?

When people ask me, "Is there one prayer that works every time…a kind of ultimate prayer?" my answer is an unequivocal, "Yes, there is."

I call it The Secret Prayer.

Does this mean other kinds of prayers don't work? Not at all. It simply means that over time I've learned that certain elements seem to get the results I desire when I pray. And I've noticed that, when others use this formula, it works for them, too.

The Secret Prayer three-step formula is based on just three things:

Step One—Active Gratitude
Step Two—Detached Request
Step Three—Inspired Action

THE SECRET PRAYER

My take on prayer is that you have to come from gratitude, not begging, and from a sincere place of thankfulness. You can make non-demand requests, but you need that spirit of letting go with trust and faith. In other words, "Not my will, but thine" becomes the foundation.

In my view, beginning with a spirit of gratitude is the core issue. In fact, if I had a one-step formula of prayer, this would be it.

Gratitude is the key to opening all doors. Saying thanks for specific things, meaning it, and feeling it is the launching pad. For example, my talking to angels throughout the day is giving thanks before going on to the next step. Sitting in my hot tub in the evening is giving prayers of thanks. If we all felt more gratitude for what we have, even the things we complain about, we'd shift our focus, our minds, our thoughts, our energies, our spirits, our directions, our actions, and more.

This first step is crucial. Gratitude for the now is the number one way to begin any prayer. It's an acknowledgement of the miracle that is already here: this moment. When you sincerely do it and feel it, you can stop with this step, too. It's that powerful. If we simply did this, all else would fall into place.

But we humans like to mess with the kitchen, so…

Requesting how you'd like it to be, without demanding it, is the second key.

Demanding is a child stomping his feet. Like begging,

THE THREE-STEP FORMULA

your ego wants a certain outcome. It pretends to know it all. But it doesn't. We barely know a tiny percentage of what's happening in our personal world at any one time. We simply can't know the big picture or the whole story.

A wiser approach is to make a request but acknowledge that something better may be more appropriate. Requesting is saying, "This would be cool, but maybe you (being all wiser) have a better idea." It needs to be playful, not desperate. It's window-shopping and wishing. It's realizing life is grand as is, but it'd be even grander if a few things were tweaked.

At the same time, when you make requests, it's important to know something better may be coming. You can do this by ending your requests with the phrase "this or something better." This requires faith.

The final step is to surrender and let go while acting on the insights, inspiration, and intuition you receive. We co-create results. The Higher Power (God, Divine, Universe, whatever name you call it) works *through* you.

When you receive an inspiration, act on it.

When you see an opportunity, seize it, even when there's no clear evidence where it will lead.

As in *The Attractor Factor*, it's the last step where you let go of psychological attachment, but you also take inspired actions. The Divine works through you, so you can't just sit. *You are the missing ingredient in most results from prayer.*

Remember the famous joke about the man who

prayed to win the lottery but was reminded to buy a ticket?

Don't be that guy...

Part of the reason I believe that The Secret Prayer formula is so effective is that it places you—the pray-*er*—into a mode to actually *receive* answers. You can pray all you want, but if you are not receptive, you may not even notice there was an answer. Each of these steps is really about you, the pray-er. They're attitudes that you bring into your prayer, which raise your energy and vibration.

You are literally uplifted by them.

What better way to sync yourself with the Law of Attraction?

THE HARDEST PRAYER

Money doesn't have beliefs about you. You have beliefs about money.

—Dr. Joe Vitale

What's the hardest prayer of all?

Ever since I began teaching people the Hawaiian healing prayer of *Ho'oponopono*—which is basically saying, "I love you, I'm sorry, please forgive me, and thank you"—I've heard the same complaints.

"I don't want to say 'I'm sorry!'"

"Why should I ask for forgiveness? I didn't do anything wrong!"

It appears that the hardest prayer of all is to request forgiveness. The great irony is this: until you forgive yourself and everyone else, you will remain stuck in the same unconscious patterns and same life experiences. You won't be able to allow much good in your life because your walls and blinders will prevent it from coming in. You have to let go, give thanks, and be here now to truly experience the miracle. And I mean *THE* MIRACLE.

Let me explain.

In the Ho'oponopono tradition, you say, "I'm sorry" and

"please forgive me" not because you did anything wrong, but because you were unconscious to what you did or didn't do. In other words, our habits, mindsets, paradigms, and hidden beliefs are operating us like puppets. Most of what we do is based on past programming, not present awareness. We are not to blame. But we are responsible.

Requesting a cleansing from the Divine is admitting our unconsciousness. All we are really saying is, "I'm sorry for being unconscious of my beliefs about money" (if you had a money issue) or "Please forgive me for my hidden patterns preventing me from attracting my life partner" (if you had a romance issue). Again, you aren't feeling guilty and you aren't blaming yourself. Instead, you are waking up to the disconnect between you and the Divine.

Said another way, prayer isn't about changing the mind of the Universe, but about changing *your* mind to be aligned with the Universe.

I want to be sure I am clear here. Throughout my research into prayer and body-mind-spirit teachings, the common thread is one word: forgiveness.

Until we forgive, we aren't aligned with the miracle of this moment.

Until we forgive, we can't see the blessings we are already receiving.

Until we forgive, we are burning up our own energy system with resentment.

Until we forgive, we are punishing ourselves in the

THE HARDEST PRAYER

hope that it will somehow punish another.

I realize forgiveness can be difficult. Everyone you know has a story of being hurt, betrayed, violated, disappointed, and more. But our pain isn't helping our present. Our pain is keeping the story alive, and the story is preventing the miracle of right now.

As beloved author Marianne Williamson has said, "Forgiveness is not always easy. At times, it feels more painful than the wound we suffered, to forgive the one that inflicted it. And yet, there is no peace without forgiveness."

The first step in The Secret Prayer is based on gratitude, but you may have trouble feeling grateful if you are still feeling hurt, or even hate. I know it's easy for me to sit here and write the words "just let it go." I know you are the one that has to do the letting go. My reminder is to weigh the cost of carrying the grudge. If you can logically realize that lack of forgiveness is stopping your joy, then you might release the pain right now.

As the great Swiss psychologist Carl Jung once wrote, "I am not what happened to me, I am what I choose to become."

You get to choose, too. Don't look back. You're not going that way. Look forward. You're going into the future, created from what you think and feel right now.

But if you need a little more help, consider this prayer:

I am grateful for my life, my body, my mind, my spirit, and

my connection to the Great Something that keeps us all alive and well.
I lovingly request that my old pains be healed and my resentment be released, that I am helped to let go of any and all resentment.
I promise to follow the inspirations and opportunities I see to help me let go of all hurts, so I can be free to experience the miracle of this moment.
Thank you, thank you, thank you.

The miracle of life is right now. That's why the first step is about gratitude. Feel thankful—genuinely thankful—for all in your life, including the people and things you'd like to change, and you merge with the greatest power of all: Divinity.

As someone once said, "If you aren't happy right now, you're missing a great opportunity!"

THE SECOND STEP: DETACHED REQUEST

A joke...

People take prayer too seriously. Essentially, you're just talking to yourself. But it's the only socially acceptable form of insanity. Not that prayer is insane. It actually seems like there's a meditative, calming effect when you say, "Please, please, please, please, please, please, please, please, please, please?"

HOW COOL IS THAT?

Prayer is when you talk to God. Meditation is when you're listening. Playing the piano allows you to do both at the same time.

—Kelsey Grammer

Let's assume for a moment you've stopped making excuses, stopped complaining, and are focused on what you have with gratitude.

Now what?

How about some fun?

That's what this next step—Requesting—is all about, and you'll want to bring a spirit of play to it. From the feeling of total gratitude, you begin to daydream about what you'd prefer. Then, while appreciating what you have, you say:

"Wouldn't it be cool if, in my next moments, I attracted [fill in the blank]?"

Do you want more income, a better job, your own business, a romantic relationship, greater health, or a new home? The trick is that it's much easier to create when you're feeling good about what you already have. It's similar to getting a job: usually people find work faster if they're already employed.

It's the same idea—like attracts like and having attracts having.

When you're in gratitude for all you have, it's as though the Divine says, "Oh, I'm glad you're enjoying that. I'll send more. In fact, I think you'll like this even better."

Step two is where people often make the mistake of getting too serious, which tends to have a balloon-popping effect. Only *you're* the balloon. What you want to do is keep yourself on the same energy level as gratitude, which comes from a playful spirit. It won't feel like that if you're bogged down in seriousness. "Wouldn't it be cool if…" is much lighter and more fun than demanding, "This is what I want," and it's this playfulness that releases the energy for your request to manifest faster.

Sometimes I'll be talking with someone who thinks they understand everything about attracting and then, at some point, they say something like, "I need to attract this amount of money by Saturday."

Just like that, their whole energy changes.

When this happens, I immediately ask them, "Why is that demand there?" It's there because somewhere, somehow, they're telling themselves that it may not work. They have a belief lodged in their unconscious mind that says, "I might not get the money and something bad will happen."

It's amazing how much those three little words, "I

need to…" can reveal about your hidden beliefs. Usually, you can release them simply by becoming aware. You realize, "Hey, if I miss a payment, I can work it out. It'll be all right."

Of course, there could also be other more complicated layers of beliefs going on here that you're not aware of such as, "I don't deserve it," or "I don't want the money to come in because money is bad." The paradox is that releasing the belief allows the thing you want to come in, but you have to take the energy of desperation out first.

This reminds me of a story about a friend whose young daughter went to pre-school. Whenever one of the children hurt or hit a playmate, the teacher would say to the offending child, "Give him (or her) a nice touch," and he'd reach out to gently pat or stroke their friend on the arm or hand, like they would a small kitten or puppy—and off they'd go to play together again.

You give your requests a "nice touch" when you use language that frees you to be playful.

Do you want a raise? Say, "Wouldn't it be cool if I got the raise on Friday?" A car? Say, "Wouldn't it be cool if I got the car that I'm imagining next month?"

When you place your requests to the Divine this way, you play with possibilities while keeping a sense of detachment, trust, and faith, and let all of that revolve around the feeling of what you would like to have. Bringing the right attitude to your requests is really the million-dollar secret for manifesting miracles.

THE SECRET PRAYER

It's a mind shift.
Now that you know this—how cool can you stand it?

PRAY FOR ANGELIC HELP

Most angels are unemployed. We don't ask them to do anything.

—Dr. Joe Vitale

One day I told a friend that I made it rain.

"Oh yeah?" she said.

"Yeah," I quickly replied. "The lawn needed it three days ago, so I put in my request for it. It didn't rain the first two days, but it did today. So there."

"Do you think maybe it was a coincidence?"

"Well, would you like me to make another coincidence for you?"

She eyed me, wondering if I was kidding or not.

I wasn't.

"Yeah, make it rain again," she challenged.

Now keep in mind I live in Central Texas, where it is typically hot and humid and, for the last few years, rain has been scarce. Our lakes are so low that you can walk across them.

And just a few years earlier, the Texas wildfires destroyed thousands of acres and homes. I was flying back from Ohio during that time, and saw the fires from

THE SECRET PRAYER

the sky. It was a wall of flame. It was surreal. It looked like a Hollywood disaster movie, but it was real.

So making it rain in Texas is a big deal these days. And my saying I had something to do with it was courageous and outrageous.

Of course, I had little to do with it.

All I did was put in a detached request—step two in The Secret Prayer formula—and wait for the rest to happen.

Here's how I do it: I've learned to enlist the help of my angels.

I believe each of us has angels hanging around, waiting for us to ask them to do something. We can't see them and they can't read our thoughts, so we have to speak what we desire. Even today, at age ninety, my father talks to his angels and insists that the only way to do it is out loud. "They can't read your mind," he says.

So I usually call out my angels and say something along the lines of, "Dear angels, I request the most benevolent outcome for our need for rain today. Please give us rain. Thank you, thank you, thank you."

You'll notice that I first get my angels' attention by declaring I want something from them. I then make my request, doing my best to be clear and direct. I also use the word "benevolent" because I want the outcome for the highest good of all. And I end with three thank yous as my code for signing off with gratitude.

I use this prayer every day, always for something that

PRAY FOR ANGELIC HELP

I'm intending for that day. My intention is always a "loose" request because I'd rather be inspired than restricted by my own intention. I want the Divine to know I'm open to something better that I may not see in the moment.

For example, when I was driving to the recording studio to begin my first album of saxophone music, I prayed for guidance. It went something like this:

"Hey angels, I request the most benevolent outcome for my sax playing in the studio today. I want to play easily and effortlessly, masterfully and with confidence and inspiration. This or something better. Thank you, thank you, thank you."

I said it out loud, of course. I felt the good vibe of a well-stated prayer, and I let it go. I trusted. I had faith. I didn't worry, doubt, or second-guess myself or my prayer or my angels.

And in the studio, I played with such joy that my producer, Daniel Barrett, beamed a big smile. At one point he was so moved by my playing that he turned on his video camera and filmed a few minutes of me swinging with my baritone saxophone.

Daniel said, "You have an almost supernatural connection with the sax."

My prayer came true. I created an album of saxophone music; complete with original hypnotic poems I was inspired to record. It's called *Afflatus*.

When I prayed for rain, I used the same template to enlist my angels' help. I called them forth, asked for the most benevolent outcome, and let it go after my three thank yous.

Did it rain?

Let me stop and ask you an important question: What do you think?

Do you think it rained?

Do you believe angels heard my request and made the skies open?

Your answer is important because it helps reveal what you truly believe about prayer.

If you said, "Yes! I believe it rained!" then you probably have strong faith that all your prayers will be heard.

If you said, "No, I don't think it rained," or even "I don't know if it rained or not," you are showing low faith on the belief barometer.

The point isn't whether it actually rained or not as a result of my prayer, but whether you believe it did?

Where do you stand? As you think about this chapter and my specific prayer for rain, do you believe it rained as a result?

COWBOY PRAYERS

They're a prayin' bunch. Ain't no two ways about it.
—Ree Drummond

My neck of the woods is cowboy country in an off-Nashville music, Whole Foods, boots and spurs kind of way. Besides the music, people are often attracted to Austin because of its underlying "New Age" component, which is best expressed in the saying, "Keep Austin weird."

That's Austin—the rest of Texas is pretty straightforward, much as you might expect it to be—plenty of old country music, big cowboy hats, and boots and spurs that actually have a job to do out on the ranch.

At first glance, Austin and the rest of Texas appear as different environments, and in certain respects, they are. Austin, I've discovered, doesn't have a corner on the spiritual realm. Cowboys do, too. In fact, they have their own church.

Cowboy church. It's true.

With over 200 of them in Texas alone, these Sunday meetings are generally held in places like rodeo arenas, barns, and other western buildings, and they often get

THE SECRET PRAYER

baptized in stock tanks that are used to provide drinking water for horses and cattle.

And that's not all...they also have their own genre of prayer, as real and plainspoken as a cowboy. While I'm sure there are untold numbers of private prayers that we'll never hear uttered aloud, in my research, I ran across a number of well-known ones, some that read like poetry, and some that are poetry.

For the most part, they don't leave anything to the imagination. For example:

May your horse never stumble,
Your spurs never rust,
Your guts never grumble,
And your cinch never bust.
May your boots never pinch,
Your crops never fail,
May you eat lots of beans,
And stay out of jail.

—Author Unknown

Probably one of the most famous is *A Cowboy's Prayer*, written by Badger Clark and first published in 1906. Over the years, it became the inspiration for many a "singing cowboy."

A Cowboy's Prayer
Oh Lord, I've never lived where churches grow.

I love creation better as it stood
That day You finished it so long ago
And looked upon Your work and called it good.
I know that others find You in the light
That's sifted down through tinted window panes,
And yet I seem to feel You near tonight
In this dim, quiet starlight on the plains.
I thank You, Lord, that I am placed so well,
That You have made my freedom so complete;
That I'm no slave of whistle, clock, or bell,
Nor weak-eyed prisoner of wall and street.
Just let me live my life as I've begun
And give me work that's open to the sky;
Make me a pardner of the wind and sun,
And I won't ask a life that's soft or high.
Let me be easy on the man that's down;
Let me be square and generous with all.
I'm careless sometimes, Lord, when I'm in town,
But never let 'em say I'm mean or small!
Make me as big and open as the plains,
As honest as the hawse between my knees,
Clean as the wind that blows behind the rains,
Free as the hawk that circles down the breeze!
Forgive me, Lord, if sometimes I forget.
You know about the reasons that are hid.
You understand the things that gall and fret;
You know me better than my mother did.
Just keep an eye on all that's done and said

THE SECRET PRAYER

And right me, sometimes, when I turn aside,
And guide me on the long, dim, trail ahead
That stretches upward toward the Great Divide.

This idea of a cowboy's prayer has caught the attention of many country singers over the years and brought it into the realm of American imagination through both music albums and film scores. A quick search of the Internet will bring up many versions that have the same or similar title—lyrics about everything from horses to women to staying alive.

And who hasn't seen Jimmy Stewart in the western movie classic, *Shenandoah* where he prays with his family at mealtime?

Lord, We cleared this land. We plowed it, sowed it, and harvested. We cooked the harvest. It wouldn't be here, we wouldn't be eatin' it if we hadn't done it all ourselves. We worked dog-bone hard for every crumb and morsel, but we thank you just the same anyway, Lord, for this food we're about to eat. Amen

One thing about those cowboys, they spend a lot of time outdoors. Their life depends on nature in a way most of us typing away on our computers in offices will never experience. The cowboys' connection with the Infinite and, at the same time, sense of mortality ever rides with them as they work and roam.

COWBOY PRAYERS

Roy Rogers, one of the most famous cowboy performers in American culture and known for his charismatic television show, recited this poem at all his Rider's Club meetings. Imagine thousands of young fans and viewers hearing and tuning in to this:

The Cowboy's Prayer

Oh Lord, I reckon I'm not much just by myself.
I fail to do a lot of things I ought to do.
But Lord, when trails are steep and passes high,
Help me ride it straight the whole way through.
And when in the falling dusk I get the final call,
I do not care how many flowers they send—
Above all else the happiest trail would be
For You to say to me, "Let's ride, My friend."
                Amen

Cowboys also say prayers at rodeo events, which are as unique to cowboy culture as ten-gallon hats. Clem McSpadden, whose great uncle was humorist Will Rogers, officiated at rodeos around the country for over sixty years. He was known as "the voice of professional rodeo." According to the *New York Times*, whenever he opened a rodeo, "he presided over a quiet moment, reciting the cowboy's prayer he had written. It became a signature of his persona."

Here's Clem's version of a cowboy's prayer.

THE SECRET PRAYER

A Cowboy's Prayer

Our gracious and heavenly Father,
We pause in the midst of this festive occasion, mindful and thoughtful of the guidance that you have given us.
As cowboys, Lord, we don't ask for any special favors, we ask only that you let us compete in this arena, as in life's arena.
We don't ask to never break a barrier, or to draw a round of steer that's hard to throw, or a chute fighting horse, or a bull that is impossible to ride.
We only ask that you help us to compete as honest as the horses we ride and in a manner as clean and pure as the wind that blows across this great land of ours.
So when we do make that last ride that is inevitable for us all to make, to that place up there, where the grass is green and lush and stirrup high, and the water runs cool, clear, and deep—
You'll tell us as we ride in—that our entry fees have been paid.
These things we ask—Amen.

I have to say that of all things to be admired in these prayers, it's the simplicity and clarity of expression in what they want. They're not asking for anything special, just that they can continue to do what they feel most inspired to do. No embellishment, no striving for the impossible (not that there's anything wrong with that), only to be granted the will to do and to live according to what is set before them.

And when it's time to lay it all down or, as they say, "make that final ride," that's okay, too. They accept and live with the facts and risks of the trade—of life itself.

In their own way, they're saying, "Not my will, but thine be done."

PRAY AND ATTRACT ROMANCE

The world is a reflection of your inner beliefs. To attract something new, change your inner world, not the mirror.
—Dr. Joe Vitale

The number one question I receive the most from readers is something along the lines of, "I'm in love with this person at work, so how can I attract him/her to me?" Variations of the question are, "My spouse left me. How can I get him back?" Or "My lover said she doesn't love me anymore, but I still love her so how can I attract her back to me?"

What these people are doing is living in a limited view of the world. After all, there are at least seven *billion* people on the planet. Surely there is someone on the planet that is a match to them.

When you pray for a particular person, you are coming from your ego. Your wonderful ego thinks it knows. It even feels like it knows. But it doesn't. It can't. With billions of people running around, many single and available, it would be impossible for it to know.

But the Divine knows.

Years ago, a woman I know decided she wanted to

find her perfect romantic partner. She did something wise. She made a list of all the qualities she wanted in the person. She didn't make a list of people. Instead, she listed the qualities she wanted in her ideal person. That list became her prayer. Because she had a clear request, she found her partner a few months later. They married and are still married today.

Back in 1912, Emmett Fox coined the phrase "mental equivalent." He wrote about it in a little booklet in 1932 that is still in print today. In short, Fox suggested that you form an image in your mind of what you want. This image is the inner reality or representation of what is desired. The image is the mental equivalent of what you want to attract.

Fox wrote, "About twenty years ago I coined the phrase 'mental equivalent.' And now I want to say that for anything that you want in your life—a healthy body, a satisfactory vocation, friends, opportunities, and above all the understanding of God—you must furnish a mental equivalent. Supply yourself with a mental equivalent, and the thing must come to you."

In short, to pray for romance is to request a person with the qualities you admire the most. Think of all the people you know or have known. Write down the characteristics you love the most in each. That list is the beginning of your mental equivalent.

Then flesh out the description in your mind. Get a sense of what the person might be like. You might not

PRAY AND ATTRACT ROMANCE

be able to put an actual name or face to the image. That's right. You don't want to focus on a person. You want the Divine to hear your prayer and then begin the process for you both to meet. Like my friend who made her list, you will soon be brought together.

But it begins right now, with the mental equivalent of what you desire. And keep in mind that you still need to work all three steps in the Secret Prayer:

- Be grateful for your life and everyone in it.
- State a detached request (mental equivalent).
- Take inspired action.

So look around and find thankfulness for what you already have, as you pray for what you want with the mental equivalent in mind, and then take action on the ideas and opportunities that come your way.

Do this and you will certainly pray romance into your life.

THE PRAYER WHEEL

A goal should scare you a little and excite you a lot.

—Dr. Joe Vitale

What's an easy way to keep your prayers on your mind?

What's easier than repeating your prayers all day long?

One solution is with a Prayer Wheel.

A Prayer Wheel is an ancient concept, probably first found in Buddhist form in China. It is still used today. A prayer wheel can be as small as a dog food can or a thimble and as large as a whiskey barrel or an oil drum. Anything goes, in truth.

The idea behind a prayer wheel is to have a visual that represents your prayers. In traditional thought, that means the prayers are written on the wheel. When you look at the wheel, whether it sits or turns, you see your prayers. When the wheel actually turns, like a clock, every revolution counts as a prayer spoken.

There's more to this than what meets the eye, of course. The visual on the wheel communicates to your brain, which we know today is how we manifest our lives. We don't create from the outside in; we create from the inside out. In other words, your outer reality is first pictured within yourself. You are a movie projector and all you see around you is being beamed from within your mind.

When you look at a prayer wheel, you are looking at the reality you *want* to manifest. You are stating your detached request to the All Seeing Eye of All That Is. It first enters your mind, and then gets relayed to the Divine. It's a way to communicate your desires to the Divine.

Think of it this way: many people today talk of a vision board. That's a board where you write affirmations or paste pictures of what you want to have, do, or be in your life. It's very popular. When I was invited to be on Oprah's television show back in 2007, the first question their staff asked was, "Do you use a vision board?" (I do.) Even Oprah knew it was a key to success.

A prayer wheel is a vision board. You can make a wheel and put any prayer or image you want on it. You can also make your own vision board. It's as simple as listing all you want to have, do, or be—your prayers—and then looking for the right pictures or phrases that sum up what you want. You then put all of those phrases and pictures on a board.

You hang the board where you will see it the most, such as your bathroom mirror or on the refrigerator. Of course, you can make copies of the vision board and put them everywhere. It should be your little secret, though.

THE PRAYER WHEEL

No need to post your prayer wheel or vision board on the Internet. You don't want to invite any negativity, criticism, or energy lowering comments.

One more thing: Don't be afraid to adjust your vision board. In other words, if something better appears in your experience, add it to the board. If you decide you no longer want something, take it off your board. You adjust as you get new information.

Here's an example: Around 2012, I decided I wanted a 1955 Mercedes-Benz Gullwing SL300. They are super cool, super fast, and super rare. One model that actor Clark Cable owned (and drove Marilyn Monroe around in) sold at an auction for (if I recall) one million dollars. I had spotted one at a collector's car lot and it was listed at half a million dollars. I looked at those sexy doors that open straight up—the doors on your car no doubt open straight out, as most car doors do, but not the Gullwing, they rise to the sky—and decided I wanted one.

I added it to my vision board, looked at it, thought about it, prayed for it, but never received it. That didn't bother me, as I was making a detached request, but I *was* curious. Why wasn't the car coming to me?

And then one day, while I was researching the car for the fun of it, I learned that it didn't have air conditioning and the windows in the doors did not lower. I live in Texas. It's hot here. That meant the car would be a traveling furnace. It'd be a spa on wheels. I'd *melt* in it. No wonder people drove the cars in 1955 and, at stop signs, opened the doors for air. They were dying inside.

With that new information, I took the car off my vision board. I no longer wanted it. It never came to me because it wasn't right for me. I didn't know that at the time, of course. But something greater than me did. Not attracting that Gullwing saved me a lot of time, energy, money, and, oh yeah, sweat.

So if you create a prayer wheel or vision board, allow it to contain suggestions for your desires, and not the actual desires. Permit the Universe to deliver what is appropriate for you. It may be what you envision. It may be something better. You have to have faith and trust.

Again, this is a way to work step two in our Secret Prayer: detached request.

Besides, if it works for Oprah, it can work for you, too, right?

THE THREE-MINUTE PRAYER

Do it trembling if you must, but do it!

—Emmet Fox

It used to baffle me to see people being cynical or negative. It was even more confusing when they were cynical or negative about the Law of Attraction, the movie *The Secret*, my book *Zero Limits*, or *me*. That *never* made sense.

But I just had a revelation that parted the clouds and showed me the sanity behind the madness. In short, people who are cynical or negative *enjoy it*. They feel good when they find fault with others.

But why?

Answer: they get a burst of serotonin in their brain when they feel they are better than someone else. It's a status rush. They are, to be blunt, happily cynical.

But there's a problem with that "Smiling Pessimist" approach to life. It all made sense to me when Dr. Loretta Breuning sent me her books. She dropped me an e-mail and said she was sending me her three latest books: *Beyond Cynical; Meet Your Happy Chemicals;* and *I, Mammal.* Each sounded fascinating, and I truly wanted to see them all. But I had no idea the first one I picked up would blow the lid off my mind and lead to a profound insight into human behavior, mine as well as yours.

Beyond Cynical: Transcend Your Mammalian Negativity, grabbed me as soon as I read the back cover copy: "Cynicism feels good because it triggers the brain chemicals that make us happy. It triggers dopamine by making things seem predictable. It boosts serotonin by making you feel superior to 'the jerks.' It stimulates oxytocin by cementing social alliances. Cynicism relieves cortisol as you fight or flee in your mind. Negativity is natural, but you can go beyond it if you choose."

Wow! All those negative, cynical people were actually *enjoying* their tirades because their brain was flooding them with feel good chemicals. Of course, they had no idea their negativity was a cocaine rush and almost as addicting. They just felt it was "natural."

And the more they did it, the more the "happy" chemicals flooded their brain, making them want to continue in the behavior, even when their negativity and cynicism hurt others. They were addicted to the feeling good that comes from feeling bad. The problem is, this cynical approach to life doesn't improve life.

And you and I both do it.

It gets in the way of our prayers because we become cynical about praying, life, and each other.

As Dr. Breuning writes in *Beyond Cynical*, "You may think your outrage serves the greater good, but it is just

THE THREE-MINUTE PRAYER

a habit wired into your neurons. You can do more for yourself and the world by going beyond it."

The good news is that negativity and cynicism can be replaced with something far healthier, happier, and more productive. After all, as Dr. Breuning points out, being cynical ultimately isn't helping you or the planet in any constructive way. She says it makes you powerless. A smarter approach would be to train yourself to become realistically optimistic.

It's called PARE in Dr. Breuning's world. That stands for Personal Agency and Realistic Expectations. She explains it this way:

Personal Agency is the awareness that you can meet your real needs through your own actions. Realistic Expectations are the knowledge that rewards are unpredictable, and frustration is not a survival threat. When you PARE, you enjoy the act of meeting your needs instead of lamenting the world's failure to meet them for you.

She goes on to explain that you can build a PARE habit "in six weeks by spending one minute thinking about something good three times a day."

Sounds easy enough.

I have one minute three times a day.

You probably do, too.

You can look at it as a new, simple prayer.

According to the author, though, it may be tough to

overturn an old habit. After all, the neuron highway for negativity may have already been paved and completed before you were six years old. You have to go "off road" a few times to begin to build a new path. Once you do, though, the new habit will have a new highway and your new positive behavior will then be natural and automatic.

I know this firsthand.

Back around 1974, I sat on the steps of the house I lived in at Kent State University, feeling unhappy. A couple walked by, saw me sulking, and the woman said, "You look like the unhappiest man on earth." I told the story to a college friend at the time who said, "You're just naturally depressed."

Today, no one says I am unhappy, negative, depressed, cynical, or anything of the sort. Over time, I retrained my brain to see the positive in life, and to get my brain chemical rush from optimism. Today people say, "You're lucky. You're just naturally happy."

Hmmm.

I was *naturally* unhappy once.

Today I'm *naturally* happy.

Which is true?

"Natural" seems to be something we can create and *then* it is viewed as natural.

While Dr. Breuning doesn't talk about the Law of Attraction, she does explain that we get what we expect. She says, "We don't imagine ourselves sifting the world for evidence that confirms our expectations. But that is

THE THREE-MINUTE PRAYER

what the brain is designed to do."

Expect the world to be messed up and people bad, and you'll find evidence for it. Your brain will "attract it" by making it seem obvious to you.

But by the same token, expect the world to be abundant and people good, and your very same brain will "attract it" by filtering out everything that doesn't match your expectations.

Or, expect prayers to be answered, and guess what, your brain will look for the evidence to prove that they *have* been answered.

One dopamine-triggering later chapter in *Beyond Cynical* describes all the huge topics many people complain about today—such as climate crisis, economic crisis, and social crisis—and balances them with a more objective and historic overview that proves things today are actually better and getting better.

Dr. Breuning isn't saying the world is perfect; she admits to problems that need a PARE attitude to resolve. But she says things *are better*. A cynic won't see the better, and may never see how to make current issues better. They, too, will get what they expect.

As I pointed out in my book, *Zero Limits*, and in the sequel, *At Zero*, your brain can't process all the 11,000,000 bits of data flying at you in every second, so it learns to filter out what you don't need to know. But the filter it uses is based on what you expect.

What do you expect?

THE SECRET PRAYER

More on target, when you pray, what do you expect?

Until you become aware of how your brain works, you will expect what you were already trained to expect. For most, that's just plain fear. To go beyond it, you need to retrain your brain to see something else. You need to learn to come from faith.

I love *Beyond Cynical* because it is making me conscious of how my brain operates. Much of Dr. Breuning's book draws from research into animal behavior, which makes sense as we basically are just animals with wallets. She quotes Robert Ardrey, who said, "We are not fallen angels, but risen apes."

You can probably draw numerous eye-opening insights about yourself and others by reading *Beyond Cynical* (and the other books) by Dr. Loretta Breuning, that is, as long as you aren't cynical about it.

IN GOD WE TRUST

There are three ways that men get what they want: by planning, by working, and by praying.

—General Patton

Much of American history is founded on spiritual roots—whether it was a band of people sailing the high seas on the Mayflower looking for religious freedom or fighting the early wars that established them on this soil.

In God they did trust.

It seems that back then prayers were very much a part of the public process. In my research, I came across Benjamin Franklin speaking to the assembly at the Constitutional Convention held in 1787. The group had been meeting for five weeks thus far and had come to a standstill, unable to break the gridlock. Old Ben, who was then eighty-one, suggested:

In the beginning of the Contest with G. Britain, when we were sensible of danger we had daily prayer in this room for the divine protection. Our prayers, Sir, were heard, and they were graciously answered....

THE SECRET PRAYER

I have lived, Sir, a long time, and the longer I live, the more convincing proofs I see of this truth—that God Governs in the affairs of men. And if a sparrow cannot fall to the ground without his notice, is it probable that an empire can rise without his aid?

...I therefore beg leave to move—that henceforth prayers imploring the assistance of Heaven, and its blessings on our deliberations, be held in this Assembly every morning before we proceed to business, and that one or more of the Clergy of this City be requested to officiate in that Service.

This motion was seconded but apparently the group adjourned without voting on it.

George Washington, then President of the United States, presided over that convention. I imagine he agreed with such a plan given he was known to pray morning and night over an open Bible. In fact, some felt it was his "secret prayer" that turned the tide in the American Revolution, when he led the Continental army against British troops.

During the Battle of Valley Forge, revolutionary troops were entrenched on the battlefield, freezing and starving. One day, a farmer who lived nearby brought much-needed provisions to the troops, and on his way back through the woods, he heard someone speaking. He tracked the voice until he came to a clearing, where he saw a man on his

IN GOD WE TRUST

knees, praying in the snow. The farmer rushed home and excitedly told his wife, "The Americans will secure their independence!" His wife asked, "What makes you say that?" The farmer replied, "I heard George Washington pray out in the woods today, and the Lord will surely hear his prayer. He will! Thee may rest assured, He will." The rest, of course, is history.

Many artists have depicted the image of Washington kneeling in prayer at Valley Forge over the years. And, according to ushistory.org, "There was a guide in the 1920s and 1930s who would give tours and show the 'exact spot upon which the General kneeled in prayer.'" While there is much debate about Washington praying in the open, it is well known that he was a prayerful man. My guess is he prayed at Valley Forge, too.

Later, during the Civil War, it wasn't uncommon for the men to pray together. As Confederate soldier, William M. Dame, wrote, "Sometimes, a few of the fellows would gather in prayer, while the rest of us fought the guns. Several times...we met under fire...we held that prayer hour every day, at sunset, during the entire campaign."

Here's a poem about prayer by a soldier of that war.

We Don't Always Get What We Pray For
(Anonymous Soldier, American Civil War)
I asked God for strength, that I might achieve.
I was made weak, that I might learn humbly to obey.

THE SECRET PRAYER

I asked for health, that I might do greater things.
I was given infirmity, that I might do better things.
I asked for riches that I might be happy.
I was given poverty, that I might be wise.
I asked for all things, that I might enjoy life.
I was given life, that I might enjoy all things.
I got nothing that I asked for, but everything I had hoped for.
Despite myself, my prayers were answered.
I among all people am most richly blessed.

As someone who has not been in the military or been an active part of war, I've been fascinated to see how much prayer enters into it, from the top down. Both General Douglas MacArthur and General George Patton played important roles in at least two major wars—WWI and WWII—and they were both praying men.

Although decorated soldiers of the highest order, they understood the toll war took from their men. MacArthur once said, "The soldier, above all other people, prays for peace, for he must suffer and bear the deepest wounds and scars of war."

A PBS film tells a story about MacArthur after he had suffered the "biggest defeat in the history of the US Army" in 1942. He'd had to surrender more than 70,000 troops who were guarding Manila Bay. He swore he would return for them and eventually kept his word, although by then there were only about 30,000 men left. When he arrived back in Manila, a city he loved and

IN GOD WE TRUST

had lived in with his wife and young son for years prior to the war, it was with a heavy heart to the point that "MacArthur could not finish this speech. He broke down and recited the Lord's Prayer."

It was also during those darkest days that he wrote his famous poem:

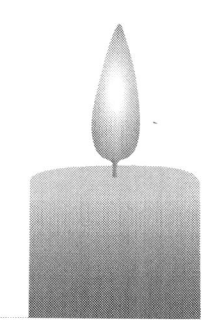

A FATHER'S PRAYER

Build me a son, O Lord, who will be strong enough to know when he is weak, and brave enough to face himself when he is afraid; one who will be proud and unbending in honest defeat, and humble and gentle in victory. Build me a son whose wishes will not take the place of deeds; a son who will know Thee—and that to know himself is the foundation stone of knowledge. Lead him, I pray, not in the path of ease and comfort, but under the stress and spur of difficulties and challenge. Here let him learn to stand up in the storm; here let him learn compassion for those who fail. Build me a son whose heart will be clear, whose goal will be high; a son who will master himself before he seeks to master other men; one who will reach into the future, yet never forget the past. And after all these things are his, add, I pray, enough of a sense of humor, so that he may always be serious, yet never take himself too seriously. Give him humility, so that he may always remember the simplicity of true greatness, the open mind of true wisdom, and the meekness of true strength. Then, I, his father, will dare to whisper, "I have not lived in vain."

There is another famous prayer story that took place

THE SECRET PRAYER

during WWII. Apparently it had been raining steadily, and General Patton called Colonel James H. O'Neill, Chief Chaplin of the Third Army, and asked, "This is General Patton; do you have a good prayer for weather? We must do something about those rains if we are to win the war." O'Neill told him he'd look for something and when he couldn't find one, set to work composing one. On December 8, 1944, General George Patton sent a Christmas card with the now famous "Patton Prayer" to all the men serving under him in the Third Army:

Almighty and most merciful Father, we humbly beseech Thee, of Thy great goodness, to restrain these immoderate rains with which we have had to contend. Grant us fair weather for Battle. Graciously hearken to us as soldiers who call Thee that, armed with Thy power, we may advance from victory to victory, and crush the oppression and wickedness of our enemies, and establish Thy justice among men and nations. Amen

After O'Neill wrote the prayer, he took it to General Patton for his approval, And Patton ordered him to print 250,000 copies to send out. Then Patton sat down at his desk and said, "Chaplain, sit down for a moment; I want to talk to you about this business of prayer."

He went on to say, "I wish you would put out a Training Letter on this subject of prayer to all the chaplains; write about nothing else, just the importance

A FATHER'S PRAYER

of prayer.... We've got to get not only the chaplains but every man in the Third Army to pray. We must ask God to stop these rains. These rains are that margin that hold defeat or victory. If we all pray, it will be like what Dr. Carrel said—it will be like plugging in on a current whose source is in Heaven. I believe that prayer completes that circuit. It is power."

Patton's comment was in reference to Dr. Alexis Carrel, a Nobel Prize laureate, who had just a few days earlier described prayer as "one of the most powerful forms of energy man can generate." It's no wonder he sent that prayer to 250,000 men.

Did he get it?

On the twentieth of December, the rains ceased and the sun came out, allowing him to win the battle against the Germans, known as the "Siege of the Bastogne." He would later say to O'Neill, "Well, Padre, our prayers worked. I knew they would."

Their trust in God served them well.

HOW TO STOP A HURRICANE

Prayer is a force as real as terrestrial gravity. As a physician, I have seen men, after all other therapy had failed, lifted out of disease and melancholy by the serene effort of prayer. Only in prayer do we achieve that complete and harmonious assembly of body, mind, and spirit, which gives the frail human reed its unshakable strength.

—Dr. Alexis Carrel

There are events in the world so overwhelming and disturbing—wars, famine, devastation, murder, and mayhem of every kind—that leave us feeling shocked and saddened. People, including me, become confused and upset. And who can blame us?

Still, I know you need to be strong in times of trouble. You need to come from inner strength and be able to help those in need. You need to choose faith over fear. And, if you really want to shift things, you need to ask a very large group to pray about it in some way.

That's how we stopped a hurricane.

Back in 2005, I asked my e-mail subscribers to help me slow down Hurricane Rita, which was aimed at Texas right after Katrina devastated New Orleans. Following is the e-mail I sent to my list:

> Help Me Stop Rita
> by Dr. Joe Vitale
> www.mrfire.com

As I type these words, people in Houston are scrambling to leave the city. The Mayor has urged many to evacuate. The next hurricane, Rita, is bigger and badder than Katrina, and it's headed this way.

Yes, our area is in the path of the hurricane, too.

With luck, by the time it hits mainland Texas, it will have dropped from a Category 5 to a Category 1 hurricane. We're stocking up on supplies, like everyone else.

While the world is still reeling from the effects of Katrina, we're now bracing for something that could be just as bad, or worse.

As I listen to the news, and watch people, the key word that everyone says or seems to breathe is "victim."

We're victims of storms.

We're victims of chance.

We're victims of a poorly run government.

We're victims of gas prices, gas shortages, inflation, recession, taxes, wars, and now—the worst of all—Mother Nature.

HOW TO STOP A HURRICANE

I'm going to say something unusual. It may upset some people. I'm hoping it will inspire you. Here goes: *You have more power than you think.*

While you may not want to stand in the path of Rita, you don't have to cower under the bed.

As odd as it may sound, I believe that if enough of us think positive, we can create a counter storm of sorts. We can protect ourselves and our loved ones with our thoughts.

I've described and proved this with the research in the back of my book, *The Attractor Factor*. Nineteen studies *proved* that when a large group of people hold positive intentions, those intentions radiate out and become reality.

No, I'm not saying ignore the storm warnings. I'm saying don't get caught up in the fear that the warnings often trigger.

Look. If you think the storm will get you, then it's already gotten you. You're living in fear. Your life is dark, gloomy, and in a cage. The media is flawless at whipping us into fear.

So I suggest ignoring the media. It's not information, it's propaganda. It gets large groups of people to think negative, which of course then becomes reality.

Why can't we do the opposite?

Why can't we get large groups of people to think positive?

THE SECRET PRAYER

At this very moment, as I type this and you read this, all is well.

Isn't it?

Aren't you okay?

Aren't you feeling fine right now?

Yes, be sure to have batteries and water and supplies.

But also check the storehouse in your mind.

Are you living in fear, or living in trust?

Are you focused on the negative, or are you doing something to create a positive?

We are all, always, at choice.

My plea is that the readers of my ezine—you—will stop, breathe, and focus; pray, or in some positive way send out an energy that will help dissolve the fear in and around us.

I'm asking you to do this on Saturday, the day Rita is scheduled to visit Texas.

As I was finishing this article, UPS delivered two books to me. Both are timely and worth mentioning.

Unconditional Bliss says you can find happiness in the face of hardship.

I think this is relevant. While the media is making us shake in our boots, we can choose to take care of ourselves and others *while* remaining happy.

Happiness is a choice.

HOW TO STOP A HURRICANE

The other book looks just as fascinating. It's *Megatrends 2010* by Pat Aburdene.

To my surprise (and delight), the book declares that the future will be more focused on spirit.

Well, let's create the future right now.

Let's focus on spirit.

What I'm asking you to do is be happy, right now. Smile. Send that loving energy out, in the direction of Texas. Intend for all to be well, for, in reality, all is well.

In fact, pretend you are the eye of the hurricane. That's the center where all is at peace. *Be* that peace and send that peace from the eye to the hurricane itself, imagining it dropping in intensity.

We can make a difference.

It begins with you.

What will you choose to think?

Did it work? Judge for yourself: Rita subsequently dropped from a Category 5 to a Category 3. It didn't even rain in my area, which was under such threat that most of the area had evacuated.

I didn't stop there. Since then, I've asked my subscribers to my e-mails and blog posts to:

• Help clean up the oil disaster in the Gulf. Shortly after my e-mail, things began to get better.

• Help stop the Texas wildfires, which had destroyed over 1,000 homes. Within minutes of my e-mail, it began to rain in some areas. We actually had a downpour over my house. The fires all went out.

• Help my dying and bedridden mother. Within a week she was crawling out of her bed, unassisted, getting into her wheelchair, and asking to watch TV. I saw her last weekend. She wanted to sit and talk. It was miraculous to see.

And there've been a few more—helping to save the Internet, helping to save the world, and helping support the town of Newtown, Connecticut.

Group intention and prayer works.

Over twenty-three scientific studies have shown that when groups of people meditate with the same positive intention, they are able to measure positive results in the world around them. When you work with your unconscious, you are also tapping into a collective unconscious that is shared by all of us. At this level, as a group, we can impact anything "out there" going on around us that we perceive as bad.

After all, we're all connected at Source.

Even if you don't believe prayer can work in cases like this, what will it hurt you to settle down for a minute to think positively and offer an intention to the Divine?

What if maybe, just maybe, it heals the situation in some way? What if it heals the Earth, and yourself, as well?

Clearly, it's worth a try, isn't it?

THE PRAYER RUNNER

On days when I can't run, I don't feel "myself," and whoever the self is I feel, I don't like nearly so much as the other.
—Joyce Carol Oates

I have a friend who told me that running, to her, was a prayer meditation. Whenever she and her husband have a disagreement of some sort, they head outside, and instead of talking, they run in silence. She said it has never failed to dissolve the negative energy and they return home once again in gratitude and love toward each other.

This made me wonder, "Is it the running or the prayer?" After doing some research, I decided it's both.

Running as a form of prayer is not new. It's been part of the mythology of the Hopi Indians for centuries. They believed that "ancestors and animals showed Indian men and women how to run, and that mythic races helped to organize the world."

As a practical matter, they ran to capture game for food long before they had horses, and they were famous for being able to cover long distances at record speed. According to one story, "In 1903, George Wharton James gave a dollar to Charlie Talawepi of Oraibi to take a message to Keams Canyon. Talawepi ran the distance of seventy-two miles and brought back a reply in thirty-six hours."

Over time, other reasons evolved to run, like health considerations. For example, the Hopi believe that running "banishes unhappiness, strengthens the body, and rejuvenates a person's energy." They also ran races (and still do) for spiritual and ceremonial purposes. "While praying as a group for rain and prosperity during ceremonies like the Snake and Basket dances, running races served as significant ceremonial events.... Such [running] games were played to bring rains and cultivate crops."

It's intriguing that running developed over time into a spiritual and health role in their culture. I imagine this is because of its positive effects on our inner being as well as outer fitness, and the fact that they still combine it with prayer events is highly telling.

It also may be that prayer makes you a *better* runner.

According to Dr. Larry Dossey in his book *Healing Words*, a medical researcher from Harvard's Medical School, Herbert Benson, found there was a positive correlation between running and praying and that "their bodies became more efficient." Using this research, he developed the idea of "aerobic prayer," which he taught to runners and walkers. Perhaps this idea was the reason behind Eric Liddell's amazing race in 1924.

Liddell was the famous Scotsman portrayed in the

THE PRAYER RUNNER

film, *Chariots of Fire,* who made headlines for a race he refused to run on Sunday because of his beliefs. As a result, he missed the opportunity to run the 200-meter race he was known for, but then went on to win the gold medal in the Olympics that year for the 400-meter race. Afterwards, he said, "The secret of my success over the 400m is that I run the first 200m as fast as I can. Then, for the second 200m, with God's help I run faster."

Another runner, Jeff Grabosky, wanted to deepen his prayer life and help others, so he decided to pray across America—literally. In 2011, he ran 3,700 miles from Oceanside, California, to Long Island, New York, doing just that with a rosary in his hand. Besides his own intentions, as he called them, he also took prayer requests for other people, gathering them through his website, by e-mail, and from those he met along the way.

And he did a *lot* of praying.

During his run, in an interview with the *Washington Times,* he said, "I have gone to God with close to 2,000 intentions, which at a decade per intention works out to 20,000 Hail Mary's." At the time, he had about one-third of his trip completed and figured he would "finish with around 3,500 different intentions."

Sometimes runners are inspired to write their prayers, as this one written by Louis B. Smith, Jr.:

This is my running prayer, Lord.
I run in praise of you.

THE SECRET PRAYER

I praise you with my motion.
You sustain my breath.
That I may sustain your praise.
All creation joining in
Nothing in creation is still.
My world revolves as I run across it.
The heavens move as I run below them.
Everything moves in praise.
I move as I run.
I run a trail of blessings,
Giving and receiving both.
As I run I am blessed,
With moisture in the air
To cool my straining body,
Plants and trees nourish my breath,
That I may run further.
With birdsong to cheer me on.
Joining in unending praise
With the supportive murmur,
Of the flowing creek.
With passion in my arms and legs,
With burning in my chest,
That I may know that I am alive,
To have more to praise you for.
I leave blessings in my turn.
Water for plants,
Breath for the trees.
This run may end.

THE PRAYER RUNNER

The prayer will not.
I may slow.
I shall praise you still.
Your praise carries me.
To the limits of my body and beyond.
Hands outstretched in praise,
I run and collect bounteous blessings.
The rhythm of the pavement sings
A percussive song of power.
Not of my might.
Not of my strength.
But of the persistence of your spirit.
A regular rhythm of irregular melody
Breath in windy counterpoint
Still I run.
Still I praise
Ever the prayer runs on.

Whatever it is that inspires the runner, it seems that it's an internal, but not uncommon, experience. In an online article for the *New York Times*, runner and writer Jamie Quatro describes this meditative space in running as a "third layer" of consciousness or "prayer consciousness."

She said, "It's a paradox: only when I'm fully present in my body do I begin to experience the absence of myself." She went on to compare it to yoga, saying, "…the more aware we become of only the breath flowing through and supporting the body, the less the stories of the self, created in our heads, seem to matter." Interestingly, this is the same kind of full body presence my friend, who is also a yoga instructor, experiences in running. They both say that the experience is one of "deep gratitude" and perhaps this is the common thread that binds it all together.

I've written before that meditation and gratitude, or any of the tools, help quiet you, allowing you to be more sensitive and in tune with God or the Divine, and helping you to feel more at one with nature. Running appears to be a way to do this easily by putting you into a meditative state that enhances your awareness of nature. The natural by-product of this experience is a feeling of gratitude. No words are necessary.

When you run, your attention becomes outer-focused and your senses sharpen. You begin to disconnect the worrying mind, which calms your inner world, allowing you to sync to the outer world. As you relax, you come into the "now" moment—the only moment there is. Now you are one with the Divine.

Who knew you could be so still while moving?

UNANSWERED PRAYERS

When the gods want to punish us, they answer our prayers.
—Oscar Wilde

Garth Brooks' hit song, "Unanswered Prayers," was based on a true story in his own life (although as he explains, he didn't run into an old flame at a "hometown football game;" it was actually at a fundraiser, but he couldn't make that work with the song). He said that for the first two years of his marriage, he believed a girl from high school was his dream girl.

You know, the one that got away…

But as it turned out, he came to realize that losing the dream girl was absolutely the best thing for him and said, "Happiness isn't about getting what you want, it's wanting what you've got." These are the chorus lyrics from his song:

Sometimes I thank God for unanswered prayers
Remember when you're talkin' to the man upstairs
That just because he doesn't answer doesn't mean he don't care
Some of God's greatest gifts are unanswered prayers

THE SECRET PRAYER

How about you? What do you believe about unanswered prayers? In my experience, I've seen people give all kinds of interpretations and meaning to them.

For example, some people think it's that the Divine has a "plan" for your life so it doesn't really matter what you think you need, and that any other route wouldn't have taken you to any better place. One man talked about his sister wanting a baby, but then her husband was killed a short time later. As he said, "God knew she wouldn't have been able to handle that."

Who knows, perhaps they are all right. Explain it any way you want, whether we're aware of it or not, things work out as they're supposed to. Nothing good comes from arguing with reality.

John Wooden, the famous UCLA basketball coach, once said, "You must have faith that things will end up as they should, which doesn't mean as you want them to, but things will work out as they should—providing, of course, that you do the things that you should do to help it become that reality."

This gets back to step three, letting go and taking the inspired action that comes to you, as Wooden goes on to say: "I think we are all guilty at times of wanting things to happen a certain way but not doing everything we are capable of to help that become a reality. We just want it to. And that's not life. That shouldn't be life."

It's true that many times things don't go the way you planned, even when you've done what you felt you should. This is the surrender part where you realize that your happiness is not dependent on any one thing working out. These are the times you choose to trust that there's something better for you. And it's the best choice because, in a world where our senses take in as much as 11,000,000 bits of information per second, it would be impossible to see the big picture—consciously, anyway.

More importantly, why would you want to when you don't need to?

To truly understand this, look back in your life at something that seemed negative at the time but now you realize benefited you. It may still be benefiting you. As author Kurt Wright suggests, and I'm paraphrasing: Have you ever noticed that a year, two years, or five years after some bad event happens to you, that you saw the humor in it or the positive reasons for it? If that insight was available from a five-year distance, wasn't it also available in the moment it happened?

Bernie Siegel, an internationally celebrated doctor who has written much about the relationship between cancer and healing, has shown how diseases come to us as gifts. Through his questioning of hundreds of patients, he discovered that the illness was serving them.

On some level they knew this to be true, although they weren't conscious of it before the question was asked. Sometimes people wanted out of the life they were in, or a relationship. Sometimes they needed a stronger version of themselves—and this was the method.

THE SECRET PRAYER

Fortunately, you don't have to have a disease to see the positive in the negative. You can do it now.

As you learn to trust that something's working behind the scenes on your behalf at all times, you'll arrive at that place where you see miracles everywhere. You won't judge them as bad because you'll know that there's not only a silver lining, but a deep spiritual reason for everything even when it doesn't appear that way. And sometimes, when the thing is long gone and the wounds have healed, you actually tell it as a funny story, or you tell it as a story where there is an insight or an observation that changed your life.

This happened to some friends of mine who were crushed when they found their dream house but the deal fell through. As it turned out, they discovered the house had mold and health problems when, a year later, the television show *Home Makeover* tore it down and rebuilt a mansion for the people living there. Even though it worked out for everyone, they realized it wasn't in their best interest at the time to buy that house and for that they were grateful.

In all your prayers, trust that the Divine is taking care of you and that everything is working out for your highest good. If things don't work out the way you want or, like Garth Brooks crooned, the one you wanted slips away, take heart. In the words of Byron Katie, author and teacher of a process called *The Work*: "You've been spared."

THE SECRET PLACE OF PRAYER

More things are wrought by prayer than this world dreams of.
   —Alfred Lord Tennyson, "Morte D'Arthur"

What do you think prayer is?

Alfred Lord Tennyson, Poet Laureate of Great Britain and Ireland in the nineteenth century, described prayer as "the secret place":

> *There is a place where thou canst touch the eyes*
> *Of blinded men to instant, perfect sight;*
> *There is a place where thou canst say, "Arise"*
> *To dying captives, bound in chains of night;*
> *There is a place where thou canst reach the store*
> *Of hoarded gold and free it for the Lord;*
> *There is a place—upon some distant shore—*
> *Where thou canst send the worker and the Word.*
> *Where is that secret place—dost thou ask, "Where?"*
> *O soul, it is the secret place of prayer!*

Whether or not you engage in it personally, most of us have grown up with some idea of what prayer is. We all come in contact with it. Even when you have no belief in it, you can't escape it because you're surrounded by others who do.

In my experience with thousands of people, I have found that most people have questions about prayer, and that this is the underlying reason for their lack of belief.

But what's there not to believe?

Prayer is first and foremost an act of communication; it is a vehicle for expressing something in you. It's about your connection to your life and to whatever sustains you here in that life, whatever you call it or however you see it. Some people refer to it as "Infinite intelligence," some simply "Divine energy." It doesn't matter whether you believe in a personal "God." You don't have to. It's about believing in good, or in something beyond.

Even Einstein, who considered himself an agnostic, wrote: "everyone who is seriously involved in the pursuit of science becomes convinced that some spirit is manifest in the laws of the universe, one that is vastly superior to that of man."

Prayer is simply a way to be in communion with this spirit that pervades everything—which means anyone can do it, and, given its power, perhaps ought to. I say "power" not because of the exterior results, manifestations, or miracles it can bring, but because of the changes you experience on an internal level.

Its true power is that it allows you to know yourself.

Through sincere prayer, you let go of the false sense

of yourself and enter into the greater version of you. In a sense, it gets you out of your own way.

According to Catherine Ponder in *The Dynamic Laws of Prayer*, "In the original Sanskrit the word for 'prayer' was 'pal-al,' meaning 'judging oneself as wondrously made.' This is among the highest forms of prayer, to recognize yourself as being a wondrous expression of God, and then to commune with that inner God-nature."

Imagine for a moment waking up each day to the thought that you were wondrously made and that God was within you?

- What would you attempt?
- What would you create?
- What would you release?
- Who would you have a conversation with?
- How would you present yourself to the world?
- What would you change?

And lastly: **How would your prayers be different?**

My guess is that, at the very least, you'd stop begging or pleading. If the Divine is within, what would be the point? Beyond that, you'd probably have much greater peace. And, if you had that, you might not pray for half the things you do. That alone would bring some relief.

When it comes to prayer, peace may be the best goal—at least for "scientific prayer" (or "treatments," as they call them in New Thought). In fact, these types of prayers are most successful when they bring the prayer, the "practitioner," to a place of peace. It's the same principle behind Ho'oponopono, which strives to help people change themselves to be at peace, not change others or situations.

This concept of working for peace within yourself is based on the concept that everything is energy. In other words, there is no place that God is not. And because it is within you, when you effect change "here," it changes "there."

So "here" is the secret place of prayer.

SCIENTIFIC PRAYER

Prayer is essential to happiness.

—Ernest Holmes

The term "New Age" covers a lot of territory.

One of the cultural movements it's often linked to is called "New Thought," which I've spent time studying over the years. But there's one major difference, as far as I can tell: New Age gets a lot of flak that New Thought appears to avoid. I imagine this is because New Age comes with ideas that sometimes stretch people's imaginations well beyond their current boundaries, including many alternative healing modalities and words that they consider too woo-woo.

New Thought, on the other hand, focuses entirely on a "science of mind."

Ernest Holmes, a spiritual teacher who wrote *The Science of Mind: A Philosophy, A Faith, A Way of Life*, helped further this movement in the twentieth century and developed a specific type of "scientific prayer" he called a Spiritual Mind Treatment.

I've used them a lot and there's nothing woo-woo about it—or the results.

THE SECRET PRAYER

Holmes understood that we manifested, or "demonstrated" as he called it, our life and the things in it *based on our beliefs*.

Sounds familiar, doesn't it?

As he said, "But right today we can expect to demonstrate or have our prayers answered according to our belief and the embodiment of that belief." To him, "the essence of the power of prayer is faith and acceptance." These were the precepts upon which he created the Spiritual Mind Treatment.

The main difference between a scientific prayer and traditional prayer was how you approached the matter. If you thought of God as "some far off Being," who might or might not answer your prayer, that was considered traditional prayer and was not very effective. To him, receiving what you desired was simply a matter of staying with an idea long enough. As he wrote in all caps: "IF GOD EVER ANSWERED PRAYER, HE ALWAYS ANSWERS PRAYER."

Nothing much left to the imagination there...

In a scientific prayer, there is no room for wiggling, pleading, or begging. The truth is you're not "asking." You're using your words directly and definitely while knowing that *your words have power*. "You are dealing with Intelligence," he advised, "so deal with it intelligently." And he created a systematic way to go about it.

A treatment begins with a recognition of Spirit as Omnipotent, Omniscient, and Omnipresent. All

SCIENTIFIC PRAYER

powerful. All knowing. Everywhere present.

"Life is a mirror and will reflect back to the thinker what he thinks into it," he said, so it's paramount that you start with this recognition of God in, as, through, and around you. Then, as you continue in prayer, the whole point is to bring you to a realization of oneness and perfection with the Divine, and to your own faith and acceptance.

Here's an example of a Spiritual Mind Treatment:

There is one Divine Life, Omnipotent, Omnipresent, Omniscient, and this Life is my life now. I am now drawing to me perfect health, perfect wealth, and perfect love. I am one with all people, all things, all life, and nothing can be withheld from me. I am surrounded by the best that life has to offer and I am grateful for all the Good that is mine. And so it is.

Just as in all prayer, you can give treatments for yourself or others, although all demonstrations and healing are based on your own realization. Because there is one Spirit in which "we live and move and have our being," the work only needs to be done within you.

Emmet Fox was another New Thought teacher who felt the same way. In Harry Gaze's biography of Fox, he quotes the great author as saying, "Your prayer works by changing the subconscious part of your mind...Every condition of your life is the outpicturing of a belief in the subconscious."

Think about that. All the conditions in your life—the good, the bad, the ugly—are "outpictures" of an inner belief system in your subconscious. This isn't cause for guilt or remorse, but for prayer. And the prayer can help clean up the mess, so to speak.

Fox went on the say, "Prayer, then, does not act directly on your body or on your circumstances; It changes your mentality—after which, of course, the outer picture must change too."

It is your thought that moves things—that "sets causation in motion."

The Science of Mind as Holmes explained it gave us a giant leap forward in how to use consciousness to think and pray. As Dr. Jean Houston wrote in the Foreword of Holmes' book, it is "for all the ages."

New Age…or not.

HOW TO BOOST YOUR PRAYER POWER

Magic's just science we don't understand yet.
—Arthur C. Clarke

Rarely a day goes by that I don't talk about how beliefs impact your reality. Either I'm writing about it, speaking on stage, TV, or film about it, or having a personal conversation with someone. When you get down to it, what you hold to be true—whether you're aware of it or not—creates your life as you know it.

So let me ask you something. Do you believe in magic? I hope you answered yes because miracles and magic are in the same class together.

And aren't miracles what you're praying for?

Is there a difference between prayer thinking and magical thinking? Not really, although please note that I'm not talking about being delusional or other psychological issues—that's a different subject entirely. It's that what I've found is when people don't believe in magic, it's often because they've lost *faith in the unseen forces*, whatever you choose to call them. Everything they "know," their entire focus, is on their current limiting conditions and circumstances—*that's* what they believe in.

And that's why I wear a mala.

My mala, made of Rudraksha beads, reminds me of who I really am. It's a reminder to me to be a spiritual being in a human body and condition, a reminder to stay connected to spirit.

According to ancient Hindu texts, these beads have profound spiritual powers and are still cultivated today for healing and therapeutic purposes. Some of their studied powers include aiding in the mental and physical body areas of:

- Concentration and memory
- Clarity and peace of mind
- Stress and anxiety
- Longevity and the aging process
- Stamina, blood pressure, heart, and nervous system

They're also very auspicious. They're known to provide divine protection, and to increase love, abundance, and prosperity.

In other words, *you wear them for all the same reasons you pray.*

I also use them as you would other prayer beads, such as a rosary. In my case, I'm not saying "Hail Marys," but the Ho'oponopono mantra: "I love you, I'm sorry, Please forgive me, Thank you" as the beads pass through my fingers.

The idea behind this act is repetitive prayer, which

as Bruce Davis says in *Monastery Without Walls*, "opens the quiet presence within us again and again until the strength of prayer is solidly with us… becomes a mantra that keeps resonating so that eventually the consciousness of every cell is touched…[and] is really never the same from one time to the next, because we are always feeling different and the silence is new each time we pray."

Historically, prayer beads have been around since the eighth century B.C.E, and more than two-thirds of the world's population use them, including Hindus, Buddhists, Christians, and Islams. The word "bead" itself comes from an Anglo-Saxon word "bede," which means "prayer."

I carry a mustard seed coin in my pocket for symbolic reasons, too. It's about the size of a quarter with a real mustard seed sealed on one side and the famous quote from Jesus engraved on the other side:

If ye have faith as a grain of mustard seed, ye shall say unto this mountain, Remove hence to yonder place; and it shall remove; and nothing shall be impossible unto you. (Matt 17:20, KJV)

I use it as both a prayer trigger and a reminder of faith, trust, and the power of unwavering intention. Just as a seed grows with water and sunlight, I know faith plus action will bring my desires to fruition. Too many people get hung up on the power of 'if' in manifesting their goals. They let their minds trip them up with questions like:

- *What if this happens?*
- *What if this goes wrong?*
- *What if it doesn't work out?*

But faith never asks the negative form of "what if?" That's doubt, not faith.

There's another kind of "What if" question. My friend Mindy Audlin, author of *What If It All Goes Right?*, suggests you ask positive questions. Instead of "What if it all fails?" ask "What if it all works?" Instead of "What if my prayers aren't answered?" ask "What if my prayers *are* answered?"

One question comes from fear, and the other from faith.

Jesus wasn't the only person to talk about the power of a mustard seed. A Mother Earth Living article about its history said that "Early Hindus…used mustard seed somehow to travel through the air…and in European history, the seeds were thought to protect against sorcery.… Carrying mustard seed in a red cloth sachet was also thought to increase the mental powers of the carrier."

I don't know that there's anything far-fetched about these ideas when you consider that science still hasn't figured out how pyramids were built and may never.

HOW TO BOOST YOUR PRAYER POWER

Cultures throughout the ages have had knowledge that worked for them but has been lost for various reasons.

I once wrote that if I needed protection, "I'd wear spaghetti strands on my head or a necklace of rabbit pellets if I thought it would help me. I think you'd be a little silly not to do whatever it took to feel stronger, from praying, to rituals, to ornaments—you name it. I mean, come on, anything that helps you get through…should be acceptable."

It's the same with any prayer and meditation tools, be they beads, mustard seeds, or something else. And they run the gamut. Here's a short list of some of the other objects used today:

Prayer Flags
Mandalas or Yantra
Prayer Boxes
Candles or Incense
Gemstones
Prayer Feathers
Prayer Sticks
Prayer Shawls
Altars
Prayer Wheel

All of these can be used for the purpose of enhancing your prayers and sharpening your faith. And without faith, there's little likelihood that you'll take any action

THE SECRET PRAYER

at all.

Why would you throw out anything that can help you attract what you want? It won't hurt you and, at the very least, you'll get noticed.

Ever since I wore my mala on the movie, *The Secret*, people stop me and ask, "Hey, Joe, what's with the beads?"

And it's the funniest thing…

As if they're not inherently powerful and historically potent enough—I think they make me look really cool.

Now who can't use a little boost?

PRAYER WITHOUT CEASING

Mind is the Master power that moulds and makes,
And Man is Mind, and evermore he takes
The tool of Thought, and, shaping what he wills,
Brings forth a thousand joys, a thousand ills
He thinks in secret, and it comes to pass:
Environment is but his looking-glass.
—James Allen, *As a Man Thinketh*

Technically speaking, every thought is a "secret" prayer.

You may find this alarming, but I believe it's very good news: *You are powerful.* It's also one of the reasons The Secret Prayer can make a difference for you.

It changes your thinking.

At first, the three-step formula of The Secret Prayer is a mechanical device to help attune you to the Divine. When you consciously use this structure, your desires don't have the effect of feeling separated from your sense of wholeness. As you use it, it will begin to reorient your moment-by-moment thinking. My friend, Will Bowen, author of *A Complaint-Free World*, has a term for this—"a consciousness conditioner." I like that.

As you practice each attribute of the Secret Prayer, it

becomes a natural way for you to be in your world. Each of the three steps becomes an active part of who you are:

You now see with gratitude.
You now live in playful expectancy.
You now flow with life.

With every thought, you are creating your life. The only choice you get about that is whether you choose to be conscious of where you're placing your attention and what thoughts you wish to highlight.

As a process, a daily prayer ritual is a powerful and gentle way to consciously practice shifting the direction and energy of your overall thinking. It opens your heart and reminds you of what truly matters, what your purpose is, and what you want to achieve through it.

It lets the Divine know you're glad to be here and to be alive, right here right now.

I recently recorded my eighty-nine-year-old father sharing with me his own "secret prayer" that, as far as I can tell, has served him well in his long, loving, and caring life. Each day he wakes up and offers these thoughts to the Divine:

Good morning, Mom. Good morning, Dad. Good morning, God.
I want to thank you, Mom, thank you, Dad, thank you, God, for giving me life.

PRAYER WITHOUT CEASING

I want to thank all three of you from the bottom of my heart for giving me life.
I have no regrets, only thank yous.
I can't give you enough thank yous to thank you for my life.
I thank you for my guardian angel.
I thank you for my wife. I'm glad you gave her back to me.
And thank you, God, for our four children: Joe, Ted, Perry, and Bonnie.
God, please, keep them healthy and safe.
I hope we never regret it, but keep them healthy and safe.
Please keep my grandchildren: Frankie, Timmy, Tommy, Nicholas, Miranda, Daniel Joseph, and my nephew, Anthony.
Keep them healthy and safe and I hope we never hope we regret them either.
God, thank you for the life you've given me.
I've had a great life. No regrets.
I want to thank you and all the good people you put around me, and God,
you put a lot of good people around me.
They did a great job with me because I'm proud of myself and I'm proud of what I do.
I'm a proud rooster and, God, I owe it all to you and the good people you put around me.
I thank you, God, and I thank the good people you put around me for a job well done.
God, one more thing, if you please…
Keep me in the health I'm in now so I can take care of my

wife.
Once you take her, give me four to eight months and then take me too.
That's all I'm asking.
Thank you, God.

Notice he leaves no doubt that he's grateful to wake up to another day, what he's here to do, and what he deeply values.

In hearing my father's secret daily prayer, I was struck by how similar it is to a poem written by Walt Whitman, one of the most famous poets and writers of American literature. Here is a passage from the "Prayer of Columbus," which appears to have been updated in modern language:

I Thank You

I cannot rest, O God; I cannot eat or drink or sleep
Till I put forth myself, my prayer, once more to You,
Breathe, bathe myself once more in You, commune with You,
Report myself once more to You.
You know my years entire, my life,
My long and crowded life of active work, not adoration merely,
You know the prayers and vigils of my youth,
You know my later solemn and visionary meditations;
You know how, before I commenced, I devoted all to come to You,

PRAYER WITHOUT CEASING

Accepting all from You, as duly comes from You.
All my undertakings have been filled with You:
The urge, the ardor, the unconquerable will.
O, I am sure they really came from You.
The end I know not; it is all in You.
You have lighted my life, O God,
With array of light, steady, ineffable,
Light rare untellable, lighting the very light,
Beyond all signs, descriptions, languages;
For that, O God, I thank You.

What about you?

Are the things of your heart clear to you, to those around you, and to the Divine from the moment you open your eyes? Or is the first thing you think about something you'd rather avoid? Using prayer to set the tone and vision of your day will lift you out of that type of negativity. In a real way, you're programming your mind to focus on what's important, which helps align your thoughts throughout the rest of the day.

As Ralph Waldo Emerson wrote in his sermon, "Pray without Ceasing":

It ought to be distinctly felt by us that we stand in the midst of two worlds, the world of matter and the world of spirit. Our bodies belong to one; our thoughts to the other.... It is not only when we audibly and in form, address our petitions to the Deity that we pray. We pray without

THE SECRET PRAYER

ceasing. Every secret wish is a prayer.

Black Elk, a Sioux medicine man and priest, said it similarly, "Great Spirit is everywhere. It is not necessary to speak to him in a loud voice. He hears whatever is in our minds and hearts."

This is the true power of your secret prayer: Your thoughts are your secret wishes.

So make them good…

And pray without ceasing.

PRAY IT IN WRITING

What can you do right now to begin to turn your life around? The very first thing is to start making a list of the things you are grateful for.

—Dr. Joe Vitale

In 1972, Catherine Ponder delivered a seminar in San Antonio on the Dynamic Laws of Prosperity, based on her classic book of the same name. She's one of my favorite spiritual authors. She also wrote *Pray and Grow Rich*, which was retitled *The Dynamic Laws of Prayer*. As I write this, she is alive and well at age ninety. I'm impressed.

In 1972, I was leaving high school and entering college. I didn't know of Ponder or her books and wouldn't for another decade or two. But someone was kind enough to post the audio of her seminar on iTunes, and I began to listen to it as I was writing this book.

Catherine is a marvelous Southern teacher, with a charming accent, and great stories. She drives home her points with actual cases from real people who worked her teachings and had impressive results.

One of her favorite methods for attracting what you

want is simple: write it down. Sounds easy, right? But do you do it? I don't always remember to do so, either.

Writing your desires down is a way to tell your conscious and unconscious mind what you desire. More than that, it's a way to put your prayer in concrete form. Instead of just saying the words, you write them down. The act of writing is for you, as well as for the Divine. It makes the request clear.

Ponder said that your desires are from the Universe. "Surface" desires, as she worded it, would come and go. You don't need to write down or pray for "an ice cream sundae." It's not a desire from the Divine. (Then again, maybe it is. I don't want to judge anyone's prayers or requests. After all, some sundaes *are* divine.)

It's those deeper, vaster, larger, more persistent desires that you want to pay attention to. Those desires—even the ones so big that they scare you a little—are the ones you want to acknowledge. According to Ponder and many other teachers, those desires are holy.

The idea behind writing them down is to make a request of the Higher Power, the Great Something behind it all. Whether you believe a prayer in writing is more powerful than a spoken prayer isn't the point. The goal is to *get clear* on what you want. Writing helps you do just that.

But how do you write it down?

My own suggestion is to describe it as having *already* happened. Rather than praying, "I want a better car," a

PRAY IT IN WRITING

more powerful statement might be, "I now drive a car I love." The act of putting the request in present tense helps you feel the energy of it. And it's this feeling that goes into the world and attracts to itself whatever is needed to make it a reality.

Catherine Ponder suggested you write your desires for each day, as well as for the month, the year, or a life. By doing so, you help paint the life you prefer.

Don't dismiss this simple technique. Ponder explained that the world is ready to give you what you request. But if you don't make a request, others who *are* making requests will dominate your life.

You are more powerful than you ever imagined.

Why not prove it by writing down a few prayerful requests right now?

THE THIRD STEP: INSPIRED ACTION

A joke...

Clasping your hands in prayer at church isn't much different than closing your eyes and making a wish before you blow out the candles on your birthday cake. You're thinking words that you hope will be true and while you wait for the wish fulfillment, you get a snack.

PRAY AND ATTRACT MONEY

No man can rise to his greatest possible height in talent or soul development unless he has plenty of money; for to unfold the soul and to develop talent he must have many things to use, and he cannot have these things unless he has money to buy them with.

—Wallace D. Wattles

Have you ever found yourself saying, "I can't do it. I can't earn money. I can't attract money. I can't get a new job. I can't open my business. I can't do whatever?"

I say pray about it and follow the inspiration into action.

I've counseled a lot of people over the years in books, workshops, coaching calls, and in person on attracting money. It's where people seem to focus the most, almost to the exclusion of the rest of their life. They jump from this thing to that thing, one shiny object after another, in the hopes that the next great thing will deliver.

It rarely does.

The problem usually isn't in the thing you're doing—it's in you.

This is where The Secret Prayer formula can really

help. For one thing, it "conditions" your mind towards a positive expectancy. It affects *you*. Going from no money to wealth—and keeping it—will most likely mean a few inner changes, and prayer can guide you to them and through them.

Certainly, it will make you wiser, and most of us could use more of that when it comes to knowing what to ask for. As C.S. Lewis said, "If God had granted all the silly prayers I've made in my life, where should I be now?" Sincere prayer can help you know the true desires of your heart. It also places you in a position to receive them as you listen and act on the signs and opportunities you're given.

That's not to say that asking for money isn't a true desire, or a "silly thing." It may be that a certain amount of money, or simply more prosperity in general, is the exact right thing for where you are. If that's the truth in this moment of your life, you'll know. And you'll know because your prayer will get answered in some way in its own time.

Using The Secret Prayer three-step formula of: 1) Active gratitude, 2) Detached request, and 3) Inspired action, here's an example of a prayer for money:

A Secret Prayer for Money
Thank you for my life and all that is in it. From the air I breathe to the earth keeping me sustained, to my body and mind operating without my conscious control, I know my

life is a great gift. I am grateful.

I respectfully ask that all my bills be handled, and my income increased, to match what I need to fulfill my life mission. The more I can receive to help myself, the more I can also help my family, friends, and causes I believe in.

I promise to take action on the ideas I receive and the opportunities I see, knowing that these are signs and clues for what I am to do next to attract more money now and to continue to live a life of magic and miracles.

Sometimes when we ask for money, what we are really wanting is more overall prosperity. We're not just looking for a few extra dollars, but something entirely new to come into our lives that inspires us and brings us to a greater expression. We want to feel we have value to offer the world.

At one of my workshops, one of the attendees asked me, "When did things change for you? Do you remember what shifted everything and allowed you to start making money?" I paused a moment. Then it came to me and I said, "It was when I decided I had value—that I had something to offer."

For a long time, like most people, I struggled with my fears and beliefs. Sometimes I still have fear when I start something completely new and it feels risky or is something I've never done before. But I understand what's happening now and I don't let it stop me. That's why it's so important to believe in yourself, and to have faith and trust in the inspiration you are given. You're given it for a reason, and you must pursue it by taking action.

My friend, Will Bowen, author of *A Complaint-Free World*, has a prayer for helping you realize this. He says it's "the greatest consciousness conditioner available" for attracting prosperity, and suggests you read it aloud every day for thirty days. Here it is:

The Prosperity Prayer and Affirmation
I am the source of all wealth. I am rich with creative ideas. My mind abounds with new, original, inspired thoughts. What I have to offer is unique, and the world desires it. My value is beyond reckoning. What the world needs and desires, I am ready to produce and give. What the world needs and desires, I recognize and fulfill. The bounty of my mind is without hindrance or limit. Nothing can stand in the way of my inspired creativeness. The overflowing power of God life energy overcomes every obstacle, and pours out into the world, blessing and prospering everyone, and everything through me. I radiate blessings, I radiate creativity, I radiate prosperity, I radiate loving service. I radiate joy, beauty, peace, wisdom and power. Humanity seeks me and rewards me. I am beloved of the world. I am wanted wherever I go. I am appreciated. What I have to offer is greatly desired. What I have to offer brings a rich reward. Through my vision the world is blessed. Through my clear thinking and steadfast purpose, wonderful

new values come into expression. My vision is as the vision of the mighty ones. My faith is as the faith of the undefeatable. My power to accomplish is unlimited. I, in my uttermost God Source, am all wealth, all power, and all productivity. I hereby declare my financial freedom, NOW and henceforth forever!

The idea of saying a prayer, affirmation, or mental treatment for a specified amount of time is not new. Ernest Holmes said that you should treat (or pray) every day until you see a result. Others have suggested repeating them multiple times a day for a certain period of, for example, thirty days.

This is not the same thing as repetitive prayer, which repeats a prayer or mantra over and over. Repetitive prayers are used as a tool to ground and deepen your devotional life and have a calming and meditative effect.

The following abundance prayer got its name after a couple won the California lottery on the twenty-eighth day after reading it in a *Science of Mind* magazine and repeating it several times a day.

28-Day Prosperity Prayer
I, (your name), know that God is the Source of all supply and that money is God in action. I know that my Good is here now. I am so rich and so full that I have an abundance of money to spare and share, today and always. I know that true prosperity includes perfect health, perfect wealth, and

perfect happiness. These words, which I speak in faith, now activate universal law, and I accept the results. I bless all that I have now, and I bless the increase. And I know that I now prosper in every way. I give thanks for this Good, and so it is!

True, lasting wealth comes through recognition of the Divine within you as the source of your supply. As you come to understand this in the deepest levels of your mind, you'll simultaneously begin to honor the value you uniquely bring to the world. It isn't even a question of whether you deserve it. It's a question of whether you'll let yourself ask and receive—and that *is* based on a belief about your "deservingness." It can stop you before you get started, as well as any other place along the path of getting something done.

The Secret Prayer three-step formula helps you change how you perceive yourself and releases those niggling, false beliefs you carry around. When you have an unshakeable belief in who you are—an expression of the Divine—you'll naturally take on more risks and accomplish more.

This is where the real work is done first.

Put your attention here…

And the money will follow.

PRAY AND SEE MIRACLES

Right now is the miracle.

—Dr. Joe Vitale

In 2012, I met a dog that changed my life. She's a Chiweenie, a cross between a Chihuahua and a Dachshund, and maybe one month old.

We already have a dog, an elderly girl named Wolfie who has a lot of pain and needs a shot every Friday to help relieve it. At the time, we also had a senior citizen cat, Nona, who has been on *Animal Planet* TV, and who liked to be the only feline in the house. After all, she's a star.

Still, I was drawn to this little puppy in the photo. Turns out, she had a brother.

I asked about the brother and learned he needed a home. His mom was a stray who was rescued and then had a litter. The pups she had were being adopted. The sister was adopted. The brother was still available. Despite the circumstances in our home, I was drawn to him. The owner sent me a photo of him and I took it with us on a trip to Canada. I looked at him every day. I used to enlarge his picture so I could look into his eyes.

THE SECRET PRAYER

Something told me to meet him.

When we returned from our international trip, we called and arranged to meet the little guy. We did and it was love at first sight. We brought him home and introduced him to the family. We called him Taco. I fell in love.

Not everyone was happy.

Our TV star kitty ran upstairs and moved up there. She wouldn't come back down.

Our elderly dog didn't like a little Tasmanian devil snipping at her face and wanting to play.

After three days of this, we realized it would be a mistake to keep him. Even our vet told us not to have a puppy. It would hurt our great-great-grandmother of a dog. It didn't help our cat. The writing was on the wall.

With tears in our eyes, we made some calls. As it turned out, the friend who introduced me to the little girl puppy told me that her friend visiting from Dallas was interested in the little brother. Within thirty minutes, they came over, met Taco, and fell in love. Taco now lives in Dallas, has a home that adores him, and is happy. His new name is Bugsy.

But here's the rub: Why did we take Taco to begin with?

Why was he led to us? And why did we have to give him up?

This bothered me for a day or so. I look for the signs and signals in life that tell me where the flow is. I then usually follow that flow, and all is well. I felt in the flow to

PRAY AND SEE MIRACLES

hear of Taco, meet him, adopt him, and love him.

But letting him go hurt.

Why did it all happen?

I finally realized that our home was simply the stop over in an unseen chain to get Taco to Dallas. Had we not adopted him, we may never have been in a position to find the Dallas home for him. In a way, we were a delivery system. Our job was to get him for a weekend and pass him to the woman visiting from out of town that very same weekend.

Wow. *There*'s the flow. We just didn't know it.

Some Divine current was directing me to do something, and directing the woman in Dallas to do something. It all worked out in Taco's favor. It all ended up being good. Even great.

But during the weekend that we had Taco, we didn't know this. There was a script being acted out, written by an unseen hand, and we were playing our parts. We just couldn't see the end result. We were caught in the moment and thought the moment was permanent.

There were several miracles in this event.

Taco got a loving home, of course. But Nerissa and I felt like we were in a Disney movie, because we experienced the joy of having Taco and seeing him get the loving owner he deserved. We still talk about Taco and how he changed our lives in a single weekend. It was a miracles fest.

Just ask Taco.

PRAY AND RELEASE WEIGHT

The purpose of prayer is not to give orders to God; the purpose of prayer is to get orders from God.
—Mark Batterson

It shouldn't be news to you that the Western world is getting fatter. What might be news, though, is so is most of the rest of the modern world.

Solutions have become a billion-dollar industry. Whether it's diet pills or new exercises or the latest diet, the world is awash with help for the overweight. Yet we remain overweight.

What gives?

I weighed six pounds at birth. Apparently I was fed some type of Miracle Grow as I quickly exploded into two hundred pounds as a child. I was overweight my entire life, well into adulthood and beyond (whatever is beyond adulthood).

Along the way, I tried exercises, diets, self-induced shots of miracle cures, juicing, fasting, and more. The list would stagger the mind. Yet I'm not alone. Anyone who has struggled with being overweight knows what I have been through. All you thin people just won't understand.

THE SECRET PRAYER

How can The Secret Prayer help here?

Once I discovered and started to practice the three-step formula, I used it on everything, including health. So my prayer went something like this:

Thank you for my body and mind. I am grateful that I am alive and well and healthy. I have a body that does all I ask of it, and keeps me working, playing, and loving. I am deeply grateful.

I respectfully request that I be shown a way to release excess weight and attract my ideal weight. I would love for this to be fun, easy, effortless, safe, and natural.

I promise to act on the ideas and opportunities given to me, trusting that they are clues to my weight release success.

Thank you, thank you, thank you.

I would say that prayer often, almost daily. Sometimes I said it out loud, which I regard as the most powerful way to pray, but sometimes I just reviewed it in my mind. I did my best to come from gratitude, but I admit sometimes I was impatient.

But then I met Morty Lefkoe, a loving, wise man who specializes in helping people release limiting beliefs. Morty helped me find and erase the beliefs I had about weight loss. He helped me lose my addiction to food. As my clarity grew, so did the opportunities to increase my quest for fitness.

One day I started to wonder whatever happened to

PRAY AND RELEASE WEIGHT

Bill Phillips, the man who invented the Body-for-Life fitness challenge and wrote several best-selling books, such as *Transformation*. His program had helped me lose weight and get fit back in 2005. It lasted for a few years. Something told me he could help me again.

I did what every modern person does today: I Googled him. It turns out that Bill is alive and well, and holding group fitness camps in his gym in Denver. I found out when the next one was and jumped on a plane.

It turned out to be a turning point. I was already a fan of Bill, but meeting his wife, Maria (who released sixty pounds in his program), and working with them both gave me the inspiration and information I needed. I went on to attend four fitness camps over two years, release fifty pounds of weight, put on twenty pounds of muscle, create new eating habits, and make working out five days a week a new habit.

While Bill Phillips was the answer to my prayer, I want to be sure you note that it was me, myself, and I who had to take action. My prayer made me aware of Bill and his program, but I still had to take inspired action and book a flight, attend the event, and return home and implement what I learned.

Believe me, if I could pay someone to work out for me and I still get the benefit, I'd do so. But life is set up to demand movement. And whether that movement is in the gym, or taking inspired action as a result of a prayer, it's still up to you.

In short, the best place to begin your lifestyle transformation is with a prayer.

PRAY AND LET IT GO

God, grant me the serenity to accept the things I cannot change, The courage to change the things I can, And the wisdom to know the difference.

—Reinhold Niebuhr

Serenity, or peace, is a by-product of surrendering, of letting go.

It's also the fastest way to attract what you want.

Did I mention the most fun, too?

There is something about being okay with things as they are at the same time you take inspired action that allows magic and miracles into your life. And that's why inspired action is step three of The Secret Prayer formula.

Sometimes people ask me, "How do I let go and take inspired action? How do I pray for the things I want and keep them in my awareness, but also be detached from them?"

This does seem incongruent, doesn't it? But the answer is in how you perceive things.

Letting go is a psychological state. When you're dependent, addicted, or attached to particular results, you're not letting go. What you're doing is a mental juggling act. For example, say your goal is to set up a website for your business by Sunday night and you begin taking action toward it. If you're in a state of surrender, you'll know that it's okay if something comes up and you get it finished a day earlier or a day later. No matter what, you're good with it. You have a sense of trust. This is how you want to be with all your requests.

The things you want are like signposts down the road. You look down the road and say things like, "I want to have this body, I want to have a marriage like this, I want to have this job where I can travel, and I want this income."

Yes, they're all things you'd like to create driving down the road of your life, but along the way you'll also want to notice any other signposts. You might see a sign ahead that says, "better job ahead, turn right" or "more money this way—follow detour," or "kiss that frog." You get the picture. The key word is flexibility.

In The Secret Prayer formula when you request something, you want to have the idea of "this or something better." Simply saying those words promotes a feeling of letting go. It's okay to change your goal for something better as you move towards it, even when you don't know in the moment what that better goal is. You're playing here. Follow the energy.

When you put too much stress on having a particular thing and think, "I'm going to do this no matter what," it can give you a heart attack, and it can hurt everyone

PRAY AND LET IT GO

around you. Your survival doesn't depend on it. Instead, the thing you want should be an energy generator, something that inspires. Once you've prayed about it, as you take action, stay open to new ideas that surprise or delight you. If your original idea morphs into something else or something more refined, that's okay. It doesn't mean you've quit on it.

You've just been redirected.

Let's say you decide to buy a new car, and on your way to the dealership you stop for gas. Someone you know pulls up and asks where you're going. You tell them, and they mention they saw an ad that morning for a new dealership in the next town over that has a big sale going on. Is it quitting if you change routes and go someplace else? No, you're getting a better deal. That's why the phrase, "this or something better," is so important.

Surrendering to the Divine will keep your journey feeling light (and sometimes lightning fast). It always leads to more to be grateful for, more action to take, and new discoveries as you go. That's the process of miracles.

Oh, and did I mention fun?

PRAYER IS GOOD MEDICINE

Who cared if there was really any Being to pray to? What mattered was the sense of giving thanks and praise, the feeling of a humble and grateful heart.
—Dr. Oliver Sacks

I don't pretend to be a medical doctor or psychologist, or even an expert in the area of health. Like you, I'm curious, interested, and open to new ideas and understanding—and from that standpoint, some things just make sense to me.

For example, Dr. Larry Dossey wrote in his book, *Healing Words*, "Prayer is not an innovation, it is a process of remembering who we really are and how we are related…Perhaps that is why it always feels good to love another, and why our prayers for others are also good for us." This statement seems to sum up the amazing, sometimes shocking effects and benefits of prayer, particularly as applied to your health.

If our prayers are about recognizing and loving the Divine, life, ourselves, and another—about realizing our connection to wholeness—could it be that establishing this relationship consciously brings forth the healing power of prayer? This is the question we have to ask.

Dr. David Levy, a neurosurgeon and author of the book, *Gray Matter*, uses prayer today with his patients, a practice that brings peace and hope to all concerned. It may also be a conscious way for him, personally, to surrender the results to the Divine. He does his highest and best skilled work—inspired action—at the same time he lets go. In the end, regardless of the outcome of the procedure, he knows that "God is good."

I don't know how Dr. Levy prays, but it sounds a lot like The Secret Prayer. Through it, he's able to operate (literally) in a life and death situation with caring, connection, presence of now, peace, and surrender.

R.A. Dickey, a professional baseball pitcher for the Toronto Blue Jays, winner of the Cy Young Award (and perhaps most famous for his knuckleball), has also used prayer to help him heal from the emotional and mental effects of early sexual abuse.

In his fascinating book and story, *Wherever I Wind Up*, he describes the intense feelings of shame and guilt that plagued him all his life and caused him to sabotage himself throughout his career, and how his faith, love, connection, and prayer supported him in eventually getting to the other side. At the end of the book, he includes his "favorite prayer" by Thomas Merton, similar in tone to the Twenty-third Psalm:

My Lord God, I have no idea where I am going. I do not see

PRAYER IS GOOD MEDICINE

the road ahead of me. I cannot know for certain where it will end. Nor do I really know myself, and the fact that I think I am following your will does not mean that I am actually doing so.

But I believe that the desire to please you does in fact please you. And I hope that I have that desire in all that I am doing. I hope that I will never do anything apart from that desire. And I know that if I do this you will lead me by the right road though I may know nothing about it.

Therefore will I trust you always though I may seem to be lost and in the shadow of death. I will not fear, for you are ever with me, and you will never leave me to face my perils alone.

You can use prayer for any kind of health issue.

Ernest Holmes wrote in *The Science of Mind* that "the root definition of *cured* is 'cared for...' As long as any cell is alive it is sensitive to care, which means that as long as a person is alive, the cells of the body respond to care." What does this mean? To Holmes, there were no diseases that weren't "curable" and much of it had to do with your state of mind.

In this sense, The Secret Prayer may also be the best preventative health measure you can take as it puts you in a healthy state of mind to begin with.

Here's a Secret Prayer example for attracting health.

THE SECRET PRAYER

A Secret Prayer for Health

Thank you for my life and all the light, love, and beauty in and around me now. From the air I breathe, to the earth keeping me sustained, to my body and mind operating without my conscious control, I know my life is a blessing and gift. I am grateful for all I am given.

I lovingly ask that I remain healthy and vibrant to do all that I am inspired to do. I know that the more radiant and vital I am, the more I can enjoy my life, serve others, and fulfill the work that is mine to do.

I promise to take action on the ideas I receive and the opportunities I see, knowing that these are signs and clues of what I am to do next to stay healthy in mind, body, and spirit. I know that a healthy life is a good life, and I do my part to attract that on all levels of my being now.

The power of healing words has been recognized throughout time. They can sooth and console a weary mind. They can bring hope and relief to the overburdened soul. And they can change how we perceive and maintain stress.

Stress may be the number one killer—who knows?

A film by National Geographic and Stanford University called *Stress: Portrait of a Killer* says stress has immense power to do damage. It can "shrink your brain, add fat to your belly, and even unravel your chromosomes."

Western medicine is catching on, however slowly, to these ideas. In the field of medical science called psychoneuroimmunology, the mind and body are not observed as separate entities—they are one. They know that if the mind is in stress, the body is affected, and its ability to resist disease is compromised.

When thought of this way, the body can become a teacher to show you how to live a healthier lifestyle because it registers every stressful thought. Prayer is not only a great way to reduce stressful thinking—to recondition your mind—it's a cheap one. You don't have to pay anyone to do it, and the return, compared to your investment, is beyond your wildest imaginings.

It's free—and stress-free.

LINCOLN'S PROMISE

I promised my God I would do it.

—Abraham Lincoln

In 1859, Charles Darwin published *On the Origin of Species*, which you might say caused a stir.

But that same year saw another book published that triggered an even greater surge of interest, discussion, and awakening: Samuel Smiles' *Self-Help*.

It was, as the direct title conveyed, the world's first self-help book. The public devoured it. It sold more than 200,000 copies the first year. It outsold Darwin's book—even Darwin bought it—and was instantly translated into other languages. It made the author a celebrity. From that point on, he was considered a type of coach to the dreamers of the world.

But Smiles was no dreamer. He was a hardworking Scottish author and government reformer who believed that struggle was necessary to develop character. He didn't believe in positive thinking but in positive doing.

One of the many people he influenced was Orison Swett Marden. Marden read *Self-Help* and spent the next thirty years—yes, *thirty years*—writing notes for his own self-improvement book. When he released *Pushing to the Front* in 1894, it became an instant bestseller. Everyone from industry leaders to US Presidents William McKinley and Theodore Roosevelt raved about it. Marden went on to write fifty more books, and began publishing *Success* magazine in 1897. He was a positive doer, just like Smiles.

Marden often used quotes and stories to drive home his message of inspiration and hope. One of his more powerful books, *He Can Who Thinks He Can*, points out that Abraham Lincoln was able to accomplish a historic feat because of a promise. Marden writes:

In September, 1862, when Lincoln issued his preliminary emancipation proclamation, the sublimest act of the nineteenth century, he made this entry in his diary: "I promised my God I would do it."

Can you imagine the power Lincoln must have felt when he kept his promise alive within himself? No amount of delay or blocks or frustration or ridicule can detour a person who feels they made a promise to their God to get something done.

When you pray, do it with an attitude that you are *really* communicating with your God. You aren't mumbling empty words. You aren't talking to yourself. You have picked up the phone and your God is on the other line.

What are you going to say?

MIND POWER TIMES TWO

The meaning you give an event is the belief that attracted it.
—Dr. Joe Vitale

I was reading Mark Batterson's book, *The Grave Robber*, when I came across a story that made me stop and reread it three times.

Batterson says the Australian sailing team was able to win the 1983 America's Cup because they rehearsed winning for three years *in their mind*.

Think about this.

The coach made an audiotape where he narrated the race, complete with a sailboat cutting through water, and ending with his team winning.

He made this recording *three years* before the actual race.

He asked his team to listen to it twice a day, *everyday*, for three years.

When the coach and his team finally reached the point in reality where the event was no longer imagined but actually happening, they had already perceived themselves as winning 2,190 times.

And, they won.

THE SECRET PRAYER

Too often people want to pray and expect results but not actually do anything. The Secret Prayer is all about doing. You begin with gratitude, make a request, and then proceed to action. You are asking "the higher power" for help, but, meanwhile, you are also helping yourself.

Using your mind to influence your reality is as old as Buddha and Jesus, but too often people dismiss it as woo-woo (whatever that term means). The thing is, mind power is science backed and God given.

I've been practicing hypnosis since the late 1960s. I know that a trance is nothing more than a belief system. When someone believes they can't do something, they are in a "trance of limitation." When someone believes they can do something—like the Australian team—they are in a "trance of abundance."

The good news is, you can choose the mindset you want to be in: victim or victor.

Until today, you may not have realized that you have a choice. You may have assumed that your life is the way it is and will always be the way it is. You're right—until you make a change. And you can begin that transformation with your mind.

The Secret Prayer is a tool to help you leave lack and limitation behind. By giving thanks for what you have, you open your mind to a new way of seeing. By requesting what you want, you tap into an inner power that can deliver it to you. And by taking action, you co-create your new reality.

I'm not sure there are any real limits in life. Just as the Australians can imagine their historic success from using their minds, you can probably have, do, or be anything you can imagine.

If that were the case, what would you like?

WHERE IS GOD?

Our wills are ours to make them thine.
—Alfred Lord Tennyson

"Do you believe in God?"

People would ask me that question after they read my book, *The Attractor Factor*, or read (or saw the movie) *The Secret*.

They somehow assumed that the Law of Attraction replaced God.

They somehow assumed that people who practice the Law of Attraction are playing God.

That confused me.

"God gave you the Law of Attraction," I would explain. "Just as God—or the Divine, Universe, or Nature—gave you gravity. It's a tool you can use, but it doesn't replace the one who gave it to you."

I'd go on to explain that I absolutely believe in God, but usually call that "ultimate force of life" the Divine, to neutralize any emotional buttons people have when they hear the word "God."

But this unseen force is not only giving us life, It is nudging us in a certain direction, too.

THE SECRET PRAYER

In a way, the force is "pruning" us.

As you go about your life, you get bumped and rocked by events as a way for Life (God, Divine, etc.) to direct you where IT wants you to go.

The more you follow the nudges, the easier life gets.

This chapter is an example.

I was sitting, eating dinner with Nerissa, when the idea for this chapter entered my mind.

I wasn't looking for an idea.

I was enjoying my dinner.

But I've learned to obey the Divine's inspirations.

So I turned to Nerissa and said, "You know how I get ideas at odd moments?"

She looked at me and said, "See you later."

She understood.

The following story is another example.

I was in New York City on business and decided to visit Rudy's Music Store in SoHo.

I knew it was famous, that Rudy Pensa is a renown collector of rare instruments, and I suspected it'd be worth the trip to see it.

It was.

The beautiful store is two stories of new and old guitars, acoustic and electric, some highly collectible, all stunning.

I was in awe of the place.

In a display case was a 1938 D'Angelico New Yorker archtop guitar.

WHERE IS GOD?

If you know guitars, you just fainted.

The late John D'Angelico is considered the Michelangelo of guitar makers.

His instruments are sought after by collectors, musicians, museums, and fans.

Books have been written about his style and his guitars.

Even Rudy, the owner of the shop, created a mammoth coffee table book (*Archtop Guitars*) with some of D'Angelico's guitars described inside, knew D'Angelico, and owns a few of his works.

D'Angelico made 1,164 guitars in his life (he died in 1964). He didn't hand carve all those guitars for fame or fortune. He said, "Big money? Big title? For what? I want to build guitars under my own name, for my own customers, the way I do it! For me that's a good life!"

And there I was, staring at one of them.

Gordon, the shopkeeper, pulled the 1938 masterpiece out of the case and handed it to me.

"I can play it?" I asked.

"Yes, of course," he said. "We want you to experience any guitar you see here."

I held the archtop as if it was out of a museum.

I strummed it and heard the sound of angels.

I looked it over and saw God's handiwork in a guitar.

I could tell the guitar was well played, well loved, and still in flawless shape.

"Everything on it is original except the covering on

the pick guard," Gordon said. "We even have the original case."

Later, Rudy showed me the ledger in his book revealing the serial number for the guitar, the year made, and who it was made for, all in D'Angelico's handwriting.

This is where I felt the inner tug at my heart that I think is the Divine calling me.

I've learned to follow those tugs.

After Rudy told me the price, and I gasped, I asked if there was a discount for a guitar lover who would probably buy other guitars from him. He laughed, ran some numbers, and gave me a slight break.

I bought it.

What does this have to do with God?

Look behind the scenes…

I only felt directed to go to one store in all of New York City: Rudy's.

I could have gone anywhere.

And while there, the D'Angelico seemed to call out my name.

I could have ignored it.

I believe all of this was Divinity aiming my direction.

Later, after I left the store and decided to walk two miles back to my hotel, I wondered what would come of my buying an investment grade work of playable art.

Then another inspiration hit me.

(Where do these inspirations come from?)

I realized that my forthcoming book, *The Secret*

WHERE IS GOD?

Prayer—yes, *this* very book—could be enriched with the story of how I was led to the guitar.

You see, I had said a prayer before I left that morning, asking to be led to the right place and to experience a joyful event.

As I've written before, "Prayer is a way to activate the Law of Attraction by requesting an intention and inviting inspiration."

I said my prayer in a state of gratitude, made a request for an exciting day, and took action by following my hunch to go to Rudy's.

From there, I simply allowed the miracle.

And it happened.

In other words, God is directing me (and you, too, of course), and we can attract (or allow) miracles when we act on the signs and opportunities we are given.

But we have to participate.

I could have said, "I'll skip Rudy's and go to Starbucks."

I could have said, "Nah, that D'Angelico is too expensive."

I could have said, "No, I'd rather finish dinner than write this chapter."

But when you say YES to the inspirations, and take action, you are following Divinity's plan for you.

When you follow inspiration—whether to build a guitar of the caliber of a D'Angelico, or to buy one—you are following the Divine's path for you.

But you may need a razor sharp sensitivity to hear the

whisper, and total faith to take action on the prompting.

Werner Erhard (founder of *est*) used to say, "If you knew what God wanted you to do, you'd do it and be happy. Well, what you are doing right now is what God wants you to do."

So the next time you feel stuck or stopped, ask if Divinity is trying to redirect your path or your process.

Or the next time you receive a nudge to leave dinner early, or buy a guitar, ask if you are ready to step out in faith.

Where is God?

Right here.

THE GAYATRI TRAIN

Let us be silent, that we may hear the whispers of the gods.
—Ralph Waldo Emerson

When the word "mantra" was originally introduced, it referred to areas of the *Vedas*, ancient Hindu scriptures over 6,000 years old. It literally means "instrument of thought."

The most famous of these, the Gayatri Mantra, is known as the "Mother of the Vedas," and may be the most revered and chanted prayer across all time, ages, and religions.

Here's the more practiced "short" version:

Om bhurbhuvah swah
tatsaviturvarenyam
bhargo devasya dhimahi
dhiyo yo nah prachodayat

This prayer offers three distinct aspects: Praise to the greater power of the Divine, meditation, and a focus on our intentions. Much like the Bible or any work of antiquity, it has been translated in multiple ways, although the overall gist and meaning remain similar. The following is from the International Sai Organization's website:

We contemplate the glory of Light illuminating the three worlds: gross, subtle, and causal.
I am that vivifying power, love, radiant illumination, and divine grace of universal intelligence.
We pray for the divine light to illumine our minds.

Each letter and word of the Gayatri Mantra is carefully arranged within a 24-syllable meter according to the strict poetry rules of the early Sanskrit language. It not only has meaning, but when repeated, it creates certain sound vibrations. Even though it's an unfamiliar language for most people, it's said that simply by uttering it you can receive its powers of wisdom and knowledge.

Some people refer to it as a "super science."

I call it the "Gayatri Train."

It's like a train going up your spine opening all seven of your body's chakras, or energy centers.

The concept of chakras also comes to us from ancient Hindu scriptures. It's a system described as centers of "spinning wheels of energy." When these energetic centers are all working and in alignment, your life flows, and one way to influence them and keep them in balance is through sound vibration. This was the thought behind one of the tracks called "Gayatri Train" on my album, *Blue Healer*, where I combine the idea of prayer and music for

THE GAYATRI TRAIN

healing.

Scientifically, music is a proven source of healing and is routinely used by modern-day health providers both in private practice and in hospitals to help patients improve. In fact, the field of physio-acoustics studies how sound frequencies work to "create sympathetic vibration in the deep tissues of the body," even down to our *bones*.

As I wrote in my book, *Healing Music:*

Rhythms in healing music are easy to comprehend because the more complex a rhythm, the more the mind has to work to decipher the vibrations.
With gentle melodies and passive rhythms, neurological pathways open to receive the flow of positive energy.

Imagine the impact of this type of music in tandem with the power of prayer, such as the Gayatri Mantra.

That's the "train" I'm talking about.

Repetitive chanting of the Gayatri Mantra is also a powerful way to bring your intentions to fruition. In this sense, it works brilliantly with the Law of Attraction by clearing problems in perception—which is really what's at the root of most people's "problems." Whenever you think or call something "bad," it's perception that's the culprit, not the thing itself. This is the meaning behind Shakespeare's famous line in *Hamlet*, "There is nothing either good or bad but thinking makes it so."

As I've said before, it's all good when you have the

awareness to see it.

As a prayer, the Gayatri Mantra asks the Divine for the ability to yield this sharper knowledge and to attain purity through this greater power's grace. With continued practice, you are brought to the realization that all things are one, that the Divine is in you, and that the power to achieve the things you want are in that one thing—your true self.

Essentially, by repeating and embracing this mantra, everything becomes clearer. You are then able to:

- See the inhibitions that presently obstruct your view of the things you need to do to reach your deepest desires.
- Focus on the positive desire to take action.
- Stop fearing hindrance, which keeps you from moving forward.

By listening and absorbing the power of this mantra, you allow the light of the Divine to adjust your perception toward the true intentions you have. Then, when your goal is identified, a clear course of action is revealed and your goals become something within your reach.

Finally, you can leave the station.

And that's why I like the Gayatri train.

Welcome aboard.

THE OVERLOOKED MESSAGE

Each of us literally chooses, by his way of attending to things, what sort of universe he shall appear to himself to inhabit.
—William James

Recently I found a one hundred year old copy of Wallace Wattles' famous book, *Financial Success Through Creative Thought,* or *The Science of Getting Rich.*

Yes, this 1915 leather bound edition, first privately published in 1910, is the book that inspired Rhonda Byrne to create her best-selling book and movie, *The Secret.*

While my computer took an hour to download new operating software, I reread Wattles book. I've read it before, of course. But several things surprised me on this fresh reading. Here are a few facts that jumped out:

• Wattles doesn't talk about the "Law of Attraction" with that exact phrase, ever, but he certainly spells out that your thoughts will attract what you get. (William Walker Atkinson made the phrase "Law of Attraction" popular in his 1906 book, *Thought Vibration or The Law of Attraction in the Thought World.* Wattles and Atkinson had the same publisher and may have known each other.)

THE SECRET PRAYER

- Wattles doesn't say *anywhere* that what you want will "magically" appear out of the air, just popping into reality before your eyes like some sort of magic trick. He stresses that what you want will be attracted through *natural* means.
- Wattles actually stresses the need to *take action* to attract what you want. He has *two* chapters on the subject. He says "the failure to connect thought with personal action" is the "biggest shipwreck" in getting results.

I loved reading the book again because I could see clearly that many people who criticize or misunderstand the Law of Attraction have simply not read Wattles' original text. Or, if they did read his book, they glossed over all the parts they didn't want to face, much like the many who watched the movie *The Secret* and somehow fogged out when I appeared on screen and said you had to take action.

Of course you have to take action.

Of course what you attract will come through natural means.

Of course it all begins with thought, which leads to behaviors, which leads to results.

Wattles explains that you have to form an image of what you want to have, do, or be in your mind. That image, held with faith and focus, will command the invisible elements of the world—the "stuff" that makes up everything, including you and me—to begin to form into your desired image. It will begin to unconsciously

THE OVERLOOKED MESSAGE

nudge you and other people to help you attract what you hold in mind.

That sounds a lot like step two in The Secret Prayer formula (detached request).

You then have to work, with gratitude and holding your faith, in the direction of making it materialize, even if, at first, you can see no way to make it happen.

That sounds a lot like step three in our formula (inspired action).

If I had to sum it up, I'd say that Wattles delivered a very simple, logical, and practical formula for attracting wealth. He's not woo-woo at all. He's psychological rather than metaphysical, also knowing what psychologist William James declared, "The greatest discovery of my generation is that a human being can alter his life by altering his attitudes," and "Act the part and you will become the part," and "Each of us literally chooses, by his way of attending to things, what sort of universe he shall appear to himself to inhabit."

Wattles' book is still in print, and copies of the original 1910 edition are available for free online. I urge you to find one and read it.

And then turn what you learn into action.

Wattles wrote: "The very best thing you can do for the whole world is to make the most of yourself."

Sounds like a worthy prayer, doesn't it?

PEACE TALKS

There are many things that are essential to arriving at true peace of mind, and one of the most important is faith, which cannot be acquired without prayer.

—John Wooden

Is there such a thing as world peace?

It's the question of the ages or, I should say, the prayer of the ages. But then, what is world peace exactly? I think this is the more challenging question.

If you ask a hundred people from around the world, you'll get a hundred different answers. There's not a model per se that says, "This is World Peace, follow me," nor are most people clear about what it looks like, feels like, and sounds like. It can be hard to imagine anything you've never seen. Given that, I don't know how it could be anything but an internal and individual idea. Personally, I think that's good news because, individually, it's totally doable.

So what is peace to *you* and how do *you* express it?

As you read the following prayers, hold that thought.

Most people would agree that in times of peace, there is an absence of conflict. Many people think of this in terms of "war," but there are other kinds. In the following prayer by Dr. Jane Goodall, who was named a UN Messenger of Peace for her continued world efforts, she seems to touch on most aspects of world conflict as we know them today and as they pertain to all living things.

Prayer for World Peace

We pray to the great Spiritual Power in which we live and move and have our being.

We pray that we may at all times keep our minds open to new ideas and shun dogma; that we may grow in our understanding of the nature of all living beings and our connectedness with the natural world; that we may become ever more filled with generosity of spirit and true compassion and love for all life; that we may strive to heal the hurts that we have inflicted on nature and control our greed for material things, knowing that our actions are harming our natural world and the future of our children; that we may value each and every human being for who he is, for who she is, reaching to the spirit that is within, knowing the power of each individual to change the world.

We pray for social justice, for the alleviation of the crippling poverty that condemns millions of people around the world to lives of misery—hungry, sick, and utterly without hope.

We pray for the children who are starving, who are condemned to homelessness, slave labor, and prostitution, and

PEACE TALKS

especially for those forced to fight, to kill and torture even members of their own family.

We pray for the victims of violence and war, for those wounded in body and for those wounded in mind.

We pray for the multitudes of refugees, forced from their homes to alien places through war or through the utter destruction of their environment.

We pray for suffering animals everywhere, for an end to the pain caused by scientific experimentation, intensive farming, fur farming, shooting, trapping, training for entertainment, abusive pet owners, and all other forms of exploitation such as overloading and overworking pack animals, bull fighting, badger baiting, dog and cock fighting and so many more.

We pray for an end to cruelty, whether to humans or other animals, for an end to bullying, and torture in all its forms.

We pray that we may learn the peace that comes with forgiving and the strength we gain in loving; that we may learn to take nothing for granted in this life; that we may learn to see and understand with our hearts; that we may learn to rejoice in our being.

We pray for these things with humility;

We pray because of the hope that is within us, and because of a faith in the ultimate triumph of the human spirit;

We pray because of our love for Creation, and because of our trust in God.

We pray, above all, for peace throughout the world.

THE SECRET PRAYER

I love this beautiful and magnanimous prayer. Each request is spelled out clearly and specifically, and it asks that love, peace, and kindness be shown to all of earth's creatures, not just its human occupants.

Many of these are not things we typically run into in the course of our day and it's easy to be unconscious about them. But I believe this is one of the purposes of prayer—to *get* conscious.

Can you imagine a world without the conflicts Dr. Goodall names? And, most importantly, how do you see yourself being a part of that?

Perhaps the following prayer by Inayat Khan can be a guide for all of us. Khan founded the Sufi Order in the West (now Sufi Order International), and had a deep appreciation for all world religions. He was more interested in his direct connection with God beyond religion, and from an early age he "would listen to the evening prayers sung in his household with great interest, and was impressed with the spiritual atmosphere produced by the chanting."

Send Thy Peace, O Lord

Send Thy peace O Lord, which is perfect and everlasting, that our souls may radiate peace.

Send Thy peace O Lord, that we may think, act and speak harmoniously.

Send Thy peace O Lord, that we may be contented and thankful for Thy bountiful gifts.

Send Thy peace O Lord, that amidst our worldly strife, we may enjoy Thy bliss.
Send Thy peace O Lord, that we may endure all, tolerate all, in the thought of Thy grace and mercy.
Send Thy peace O Lord, that our lives may become a Divine vision and in Thy light, all darkness may vanish.
Send Thy peace O Lord, our Father and Mother, that we Thy children on Earth may all unite in one family.

Notice that both of the above prayers were directed to the Divine. The next prayer takes a different turn although, given its author, has the same evocative feeling and tone.

And this one is meant for you—for all of us.

Teresa of Avila, a Roman Catholic saint and Spanish mystic in the sixteenth century, was a "theologian of contemplative life through mental prayer." Mental prayer in this sense is sometimes called "interior prayer." It is what it sounds like—a meditative, felt experience that rests entirely within the heart and mind of the one praying. It is an inner dialogue, not a vocal one. The result is faith.

The following "prayer" for peace is by Teresa of Avila:

May today there be peace within.
May you trust God that you are exactly where you are meant to be.
May you not forget the infinite possibilities that are born of

THE SECRET PRAYER

faith.
May you use those gifts that you have received, and pass on the love that has been given to you.
May you be content knowing you are a child of God.
Let this presence settle into your bones, and allow your soul the freedom to sing, dance, praise and love.
It is there for each and every one of us.

Another important figure in the Roman Catholic Church, Mother Teresa, wrote in her book, *Where There is Love, There is God*: "The fruit of prayer is a deepening of faith. The fruit of faith is love, and the fruit of love is service. But to be able to pray we need silence; silence of the heart. And if we don't have that silence, we don't know how to pray."

There is no doubt the Divine is within us all—"for each and every one of us"—as studies have shown. We are united by a collective consciousness and through it we all have the capacity for bringing peace into the world.

Since the early seventies, a number of studies involving what is known as "The Maharishi Effect" have demonstrated that there is a collective consciousness we are all connected by, and that, when joined through meditation in sufficient numbers, brings coherence to the whole. The result is everything from reduced crime to fewer war deaths to, well, less war.

Maharishi Mahesh Yogi, who created a distinct meditation called Transcendental Meditation (often simply referred to as TM), was the founder of a worldwide organization based in Fairfield, Iowa that has worked with US cities and on international peace projects to demonstrate these results.

According to an article by David Orme-Johnson, PhD, the Maharishi believed that world peace was predicated on "self-knowledge, the bliss that it affords, and the coherence that it creates in collective consciousness bring life in accord with natural law in society, creating peace."

In essence, when we become self-knowing, we become more effective peacemakers. We don't have to ask the Divine to create peace. Or to bring peace. Or for wars to end.

Instead of asking for something, we can just be the thing itself.

AFFLATUS

Many things are possible for the person who has hope. Even more is possible for the person who has faith. And still more is possible for the person who knows how to love. But everything is possible for the person who practices all three virtues.

—Brother Lawrence

In 2014, I posted this on my Facebook fan page: "Inspiration gives you a desire. Decision makes it an intention. Action makes it real."

That statement helps clarify what it takes to attract what you want. But let's explore it deeper than a Facebook post so you understand the power of it.

First, an idea is what you get a feeling to do. An idea is an internal nudge to create something. It's different for each person as each of us has a different life mission. My inspiration might be to write another book, or to compose a new song. Yours might be to run for political office, open a bakery, or raise happy kids.

An inspiration is either from what I call the Divine, or it's from your ego.

Nobody outside of you knows for sure what is right for you. It's your life and up to you to discern the difference.

With a little reflection, though, you can tell where the idea is coming from. There is nothing wrong with an ego desire, but it's nobler to come from a higher purpose.

Recently, a listener of my latest audio program, *The Zero Point*, contacted me and told me about the word "Afflatus." He thought it might be a better word for the kind of inspiration I refer to these days. He was right.

According to Wikipedia, "afflatus" is a Latin term used by Cicero. It means more than "inspiration," and in fact translates as "…the staggering and stunning blow of a new idea, an idea that the recipient may be unable to explain."

I love the word *afflatus* so much that I dedicated my latest album, *Reflection*, to it.

Again, you can receive an idea based on memory (previous data in your mind), an inspiration (combining previous ideas into something new), or from *afflatus* (a completely new idea that stuns you).

The idea should move you to *want* to take action.

As I also wrote on my Facebook page: "If you don't have some self doubts and fears when you pursue a dream, then you haven't dreamed big enough."

And that leads to the next step… Decision.

Your decision is what gives the idea power to become a reality.

You have free will, so you can ignore the idea, or you can decide to bring it into reality.

I learned decades ago that if I ignore my inspired

AFFLATUS

calling, my life is bumpy. When I decide to follow my inspiration, life is smooth. I prefer the latter.

Again, it's your choice. When you decide to follow your inspiration, it now becomes an intention. Intentions rule the earth. It's just wiser to pursue a higher intention than a lower one.

What's the difference?

- An ego-based intention is only about you.
- A Divine-based intention is about you and others.

I once spoke on the same stage as Jose Silva, the founder of Silva Mind Control. Jose said a goal should influence you and at least three other people.

I love that guideline. It gets you out of your own individual experience of life and moves you into a deeper awareness of others.

It also makes taking action easier.

When you know that your actions are going to touch at least three other people, then you are more motivated to decide to do something.

So step two is to decide.

And that leads to…action.

Action brings the idea, now an intention, onto the earth plane.

Nothing happens until something moves. You are a co-creator with life. Life itself wants you to do something. When you do it, you trigger it becoming real.

If I want to write a book, I have to sit down and write.

If I want to play the saxophone, I have to sit down

and practice.

If you are going to open a bakery, you need to fill out the forms and do the work.

This is where a lot of Law of Attraction students fall short. They think if they just affirm it, it will appear.

Well, it *might*.

But more often than not, you have to *do something* to work with reality. It's no accident that the word *action* is in the word *attraction*.

Let me give you one final example of how this process works.

Guitar Monk Mathew Dixon and myself are in the studio recording the third album in our trilogy of "zero" music. Following the success of *At Zero* and *Aligning to Zero*, this one will be called *432 to Zero*.

As is our custom, we don't plan or strategize. We "make space" for inspiration to guide us, and we are ready to take action on a moment's notice. We are in the studio, prepared, and ready.

One day neither of us felt compelled or inspired.

We sat in the studio and looked at each other. We've done this enough to know that sometimes you have to wait, and sometimes nothing will come. We've learned to trust the process and be patient.

Suddenly I felt afflatus strike.

I looked at Mathew and shared my idea.

"What if I played two harmonicas?" I asked.

"But we don't have a bass line or a foundation track

AFFLATUS

for you to play against. You'd be playing to yourself."

"I know," I said. "But I feel like trying it. If it doesn't work, we can just delete the audio file."

"Why two harmonicas?"

"I'm not sure," I said. "I somehow feel if I just improvised harmonica in what's called the second position, and then improvised playing in the first position, I'd be in the same key but the two harmonicas would sound different."

I have no idea where that idea came from.

But since it arrived as a gift, the next step was to decide to act on it, and the third was to take action.

Mathew agreed to try it.

I pulled out two harmonicas, and started to play.

I simply allowed myself to be guided by whatever feeling was welling up and directing me.

I didn't think about it. I trusted that the process would be whatever it was, and that was good enough.

When I was done playing, Mathew was beaming.

"That was incredible!" he said. "We may have just created a whole new genre of music!"

That's how this process works.

The formula is simple.

Inspiration gives you a desire. Decision makes it an intention. Action makes it real.

That said, what are you going to do next?

THE RING OF POWER

If one does right his mind should never be disturbed by anything [that] he cannot prevent. He should be thoroughly convinced that if he does his duty, Providence will take care of the rest, and never send accident, poverty, disease, or any other apparent evil except for an ultimate good purpose.
—P.T. Barnum

As I see it, there are two schools of thought about humans and prayer. Boiling it down to its essential argument, one seems to be that people should decide what they want and ask God for it, and the other is that they should just let God decide and figure it out for them. In a sense, it's like pitting "Ask and ye shall receive" against "Thy will, not mine, be done."

Personally, I think it's both—not either/or—and that, like most everything else, there's more to the story.

Could they both be right?

In my book, *There's a Customer Born Every Minute* about the life of P.T. Barnum, I talk about his amazing ability to face the many disasters and personal tragedies of his life with great aplomb: "*He weathered the storms with a calmness that most people would envy. Throughout it all Barnum maintained this optimistic attitude toward life in general. He somehow knew all would be well."*

The more I dug into his world, the more I came to understand that what allowed him to keep "getting on," as he called it, despite anything and everything that was thrown in his way, was his faith, expressed in the simple idea that "Not my will, but thine, be done." I refer to this in the book as one of his "rings of power." It is this faith that made everything possible for him. You might even say he took it to his grave. The words, "Not my will, but thine, be done," are inscribed on the top of his small humble headstone.

According to research by such institutions as Spindrift, it is this attitude of "not my will but yours" in prayer that works the best in getting results. Frankly, it makes you wonder why anyone would bother to pray, at least until you remember that the point of prayer is to get out of the way; to let go and let the Divine do Its wiser thing.

This was the idea behind a prayer I wrote and recorded for my "Invoking Divinity" album, alongside Mathew Dixon:

Dear Divine, I am grateful for all you have given me, seen and unseen, and continue to do for me. I am grateful for my life, and all in and around it. I am blessed in ways I do not even know, from the gift of life itself to all the experiences I have been given and have attracted.
I know there is a Divine underflow and direction to my life,

THE RING OF POWER

and you are nudging me to stay on my path and fulfill your mission for me, and I am grateful. From the air I breathe, to the body I own, to the love you show me, even when I am not looking, I am grateful. I request the removal of any and all blocks within me to the fulfillment of your mission for me. I am ready to let go and let the Divine flow.

Notice that this prayer is heavily focused on gratitude and the only real request it makes is to remove any blocks to a "Thy will be done" attitude.

However, I want to point out that agreeing with this idea doesn't mean don't take any action and sit there like a potato. It means take *inspired action*, and that brings up the other side of the issue, "Ask and you shall receive."

Those words are as important and relevant to prayer as "Thy will be done," and, taking them literally, it can't be wrong to ask. You're supposed to. But notice that nowhere in that phrase does it say you will get what you ask for. It simply says, "You will receive."

You will receive something...

That's it. That's all it says.

In other words, you might not get what you ask for—

[Drum roll, please....]

But you will get the best thing for you at that time. You will get either the thing you want or something else that's better (and may lead you to that other thing).

Thinking about it this way, setting an intention (step

two—requesting/asking) and letting go (step three—inspired action/"Thy will be done") are like two sides of the same coin. They co-exist in order for you to receive and take inspired action and to create the life you desire. Inspired action is what comes from your direct connection to the Divine within yourself. I've often described it as a feeling like a push or a motivation that has a sweet energy to it, a good feeling to it. It's something you *want* to do. It feels like a Divine source nudging you to do something—that's the action part. Letting go means you take the action without being concerned about the end results.

I was talking to George Helmer while I was writing this book. George was the business partner of Steve Reeves, the legendary bodybuilder and actor. George just finished a biography of Reeves, titled, *A Moment In Time*. George told me, "I couldn't not do it. Something lodged in my mind and wouldn't let go. I didn't know how to write the book or what to do after I wrote it, but I did it anyway." And today the book is published.

I saw my wife go through the same experience. Nerissa worked day and night, to complete exhaustion, to create seventy-five all original recipes from zero. They were all "breads" made out of seeds and nuts, not grains. She didn't know where all the inspiration and action would go, but she ended up creating a book titled *Bread-Free Bread*. And today the book is a best seller.

P.T. Barnum was a master at this, always taking action

on his many goals and projects while also letting go. "Not my will, but thine, be done," was his secret prayer for living a stress-free life. And it was this kind of faith that gave him the emotional freedom and optimism which sustained his high energy—"ring of power"—that prospered him all of his days.

PRAY A BETTER FUTURE

Prayer is motion. It is learning how to move toward a change in your bank balance, your marital status, or social world. Learn to master the art of motion; for after you move, change begins to rise up out of the deep.

—Neville Goddard

People often ask me, "How do I attract a better future?"

But after years of my own personal growth and evolution, I have learned a far better question to ask.

"How do I *pray* a better future?"

To answer this, I have to turn to someone who's had a deep influence on my own life and development—Neville Goddard—who was a mystic, author, and speaker. There is little I write or talk about that doesn't in some way reflect some of his teachings. Even Ho'oponopono, which I love and practice, has certain overtones that are similar to his message.

Basically he taught, "Go to the end result."

And that, to him, was the right way to pray.

I wrote about Neville in *The Attractor Factor*, coining the word "Nevillize" or "Nevillizing," which is shorthand for his method of attaining a goal or desire. Instead of focusing on a goal and imagining that you're going to have it in the future, you Nevillize it by pretending it's here now and complete. So, instead of saying "I want to attract health," you'd say, "I am healthy now," and step into it *as if* it's real in this moment.

To Neville, prayer was about "*the art of believing what is denied by the senses,*" and this held the key to achieving your ideal life. He wrote:

'Don't desire them, live them!' This is true. Desire is thinking of! Living is thinking from! Don't go through life desiring. Live your desire. Think it is already fulfilled. Believe it is true; for an assumption, though false, if persisted in will harden into fact.

In this type of meditative prayer, you imagine your life as already being the abundant, prosperous, healthy, happy one that you long for. You step into it and live it mentally right now. You don't just visualize it; you actually feel it happening.

It's all about imagination and faith.

Neville wrote, "Imagination and faith are the only faculties of the mind needed to create objective conditions.... It depends on your ability to feel and accept as true what your objective senses deny." In other words, everything you need—imagination and faith—is within you.

Where else could they be?

PRAY A BETTER FUTURE

Beyond that, Neville said you simply needed persistence to realize your desire in objective reality. He wasn't talking about the kind of persistence where you just keep doing the "same old, same old" but with more hard work and effort. He meant that you stayed with your inner activity of prayer until your prayer was answered.

Persistence is the key to a change in life—more income, greater recognition, or whatever the desire may be. If your desire is not fulfilled today, tomorrow, next week, or next month—persist, for persistency will pay off. All of your prayers will be answered if you will not give up.

According to Neville, true prayer mastery requires practice in "the art of motion"—moving in your imagination to the place where your desires are fulfilled.

Most people think in terms of wanting and longing for something, like money, and this gets mixed into their imagining process. This only serves to push it away. In essence you're saying, "The thing I want is somewhere out there in the future." But Neville says, "You can move in imagination to any place and any time. Dwell there as though it were true, and you will have learned the secret of prayer."

If you want a million dollars, what would that feel like? How would it feel to know you have that in your bank account? Where are you? How are you spending it? What checks are you writing? How do you feel inside?

Let it be real because, as Neville said, it "will harden into reality the more you do it." The objective is to make an emotional connection to your future, which will accelerate the process of attracting what you want into your life.

This type of prayer is a way to program your mind for success, to set up the radar in your brain to look for the opportunities to attract to you the things you say you want. You will be led into your future step-by-step. Neville said:

In imagination, I can put myself where I desire to be. I move and view the world from there. Then I return here, confident that—in a way unknown to me—this being who can do all things and knows all things, will lead me physically across a bridge of incident up to where I have placed myself.

In effect, your subconscious mind doesn't know the difference between reality and imagination, so when you put an emotionally charged desire into your mind, it doesn't know it hasn't happened. It's receiving an unconscious template to attract it into your life.

Everyone has the capability to use his or her imagination. You may be more visual, auditory, or kinesthetic, and that's fine. You may even think, "I don't visualize very well," but that isn't really true. For example, if I ask you, "Do you have a cell phone?" you'd probably say, "Yes." Then, if I ask you, "Do you know where it is?"

you'd probably be able to tell me. "Yes, it's sitting on the table getting charged." You may not be describing it in terms of its color or size, but you'd have a sense or feel of it. And that's all you need—the embodiment of the end result.

What I love about Neville's form of prayer is its element of playfulness. There's nothing pious about it. Once you've made something real to you, like a child lost in a dream, a smile lights up your face and you feel grateful. You've taken out the longing, the struggle, and the time delay.

It's already over. You're living it.

And that better future?

It's now.

PRAY FOR OTHERS

Pessimism leads to weakness, optimism to power.
—William James

Before we end the book and go our merry ways, what about praying for others? Does The Secret Prayer work for them, too?

Mathew Dixon is my music teacher, friend, and partner on several music albums, from *Invoking Divinity* to *At Zero*. He's also a wise spiritual person. One day he told me of a method he was experimenting with where he prayed or intended for others. I thought it was brilliant and urged him to write about it. He did, in a little book titled, *Attracting for Others*.

Mathew's method goes like this: whenever he hears others state a desire or a complaint, he quietly turns it into a Secret Prayer for them. In his mind, without saying a word, he imagines that they attract their desire or resolve their complaint. He sees it complete, and he lets it go.

He's basically using the three-step formula you have learned in this book. He starts from a place of gratitude within himself. After all, it isn't his desire or problem, but the other person's. So Mathew is in a state of peace. He has no attachment to how things work out.

From there, he makes a detached request that the person receive his or her resolution, for the highest good of all concerned. Mathew doesn't know how this will happen, and it isn't his job to know. He simply imagines the request as being fulfilled.

Finally, he lets it go. If he feels inspired to say or do something, he will act on it. But in this case, it's up to the other person to take inspired action. Mathew's job is done.

I've used this method myself. Whenever I'm talking to someone, or over hearing a conversation, I listen for what the person really wants. When I hear it, I make a mental note of requesting it be handled. I then have faith that my silent, Secret Prayer for the other will be heard.

The goal of life is for you and me to take care of ourselves. The stronger we are, the better we can help all around us. But if you want to help others, you can do so with this method.

In fact, I'm doing it for you right now.

Now that we have completed this journey together—or, started it, depending on how you look at it—it's time for you to enjoy all the miracles that await you in the here and now. My Secret Prayer for you is that you realize you are loved, you are powerful, and *you are the miracle*.

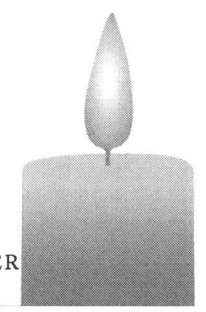

AFTERWORD
THE GUARANTEED RESULTS SECRET PRAYER

Pray as though everything depended on God.
Work as though everything depended on you.
—Saint Augustine

To wrap up this book, I want to lead you through a Secret Prayer that always works. In fact, it is guaranteed to get results.

It combines all the concepts we have discussed in this book, and of course focuses on the actual three steps of The Secret Prayer:

1. **Active Gratitude**
2. **Detached Request**
3. **Inspired Action**

You can read along and imagine all the steps, or you can record the following and listen to it as you close your eyes. You can also find a recording of this, made by me, on www.TheSecretPrayer.com.

Either way, this particular prayer will attract the miracles you seek, because it begins with a focus on the miracle you are currently living though you may not realize it.

Here is The Guaranteed Results Secret Prayer:

Relax and breathe deep…

Focus on being in the here and now. It's just you and me and this moment. Sigh and release all concern, all worry, all issues of mind. For the moment, you want to be here now, feeling gratitude for the now.

Wherever you are, notice that life is supporting you. Whether you are at home or your office, at the beach or the woods, your life is being supported by Something greater than you. Call it God, Divinity, Zero, the Whiteboard, or Nature. This "Great Something" is pumping oxygen and blood through your body, keeping your body-mind-spirit system alive, and supporting the planet with things we often take for granted, such as oxygen, gravity, and more. We are circling around in a solar system that is somehow keeping its balance. And meanwhile, our bodies are alive and keeping us here now, focused on this moment and all the wonderful things in it. The message is clear, something is taking care of you.

There is much to be grateful for, but you can focus on just one thing to expand your gratitude. It can be the chair or bed you are on. It could be this book. It could be your eyes for seeing and ears for hearing and your brain for understanding. It could be a loved one. Anything is allowed, because you have the freedom to focus on anything you want.

As you choose to focus on gratitude, and you feel the spirit

AFTERWORD

of thankfulness expand within you, allow this warm feeling of love to fill your body and mind. You are living the miracle. Behind the theatre of life, with its ups and downs, all is well. All is good. At the very Source of life, all is wonderful and you are part of that wonder. You are loved. You are the miracle.

Take a moment to really soak up this glorious feeling because realizing the miracle of right now is the essential first step of The Secret Prayer…

And now think about what you would like to have, do, or be. What would be cool to attract into your life? What would be fun?

Let your mind deliver ideas and possibilities to you. Don't judge or censor anything. Allow it all to come into your awareness. You are simply playing with possibilities.

As you think about all the wonderful things you can experience, allow one to come to your full attention. Which one of these possibilities feels like a heartfelt desire?

Pick one to go through this prayer, knowing you can practice this prayer as often as you like, and focus on different divine desires each time.

Now think of the mental equivalent of your desire.

Imagine your desire being a real, live experience. Describe it in your mind. See it in your mind. Do your best to playfully describe this desire so you can truly imagine it in your mind.

Take a moment to find the mental equivalent of your desire…

And now Nevillize the desire by pretending that it has

already come to pass. Your desire no longer exists in the future, but is actually now part of your past. You have experienced it as real.

What does it feel like to have, do, or be the thing you desired? Feel it real right now.

Take a moment to allow your desire to be a complete experience in your body and mind…

And now come back to this moment and realize that you have planted a seed with the Great Something. You have made a request. You will be given signs and symbols, ideas and opportunities, to help you bring your desire into reality. You promise to courageously act on the windows and doors that open for you.

You have faith that all is working in your favor, and every moment is bringing you to your desired result, or something even better.

To help you accelerate the process, you will spend time in gratitude, feeling the miracle of this moment, and you will be aware and alert for the things for you to do next. You promise to take inspired action. You promise to do your part in the co-creation of your life.

You can end this prayer with a statement of gratitude, such as "Thank you, thank you, thank you" or "Not my will but thine be done" or "This or something better" or simply "I love you."

So be it.
And it is so.
Amen.

PRAYER HOTLINES

This list is offered to help you when you want a little extra support. I have not checked every listing nor do I endorse any particular listing. All sites and phone numbers are accurate at the time of this publication.

88.3—THE JOY FM—PRAYER CENTER
http://www.wafj.com/prayerSubmit.php
http://www.wafj.com/
877-800-PRAY (7729)

AGAPE LIVE
http://agapelive.com/ministries/practitioner-core/prayer-ministry/#.VDc1L_ldV8E
http://agapelive.com/
310-348-1270

BELIEVER'S ANOINTING
866-549-0981

BILLY GRAHAM MINISTRY

http://www.billygraham.org.uk/Groups/171092/Billy_Graham_Evangelistic/Spiritual_Growth/Request_Prayer/Request_Prayer.aspx
http://bgea.org.uk/
prayer@bgea.co.uk
877-247-2426

CBN—CHRISTIAN BROADCASTING NETWORK—700 CLUB PRAYER CENTER

http://www.cbn.com/spirituallife/prayerandcounseling/
http://www.cbn.com/index.aspx
800-823-6053

CHAPLAIN DAYNA SPENCE (6PM TO 9PM DAILY)

http://www.dschaplains.com/
https://www.facebook.com/pages/D-Spence-Chaplains/443380169078864
pray4me@dschaplains.com
610-430-3119

CHRISTIAN AID (PRAYERLINE FOR ADULTS AND KIDS)

http://www.christianaid.org/PrayerlineForKids/PrayerlineForKids.aspx
http://www.christianaid.org/home/1/home.aspx
434-977-5650

PRAYER HOTLINES

CHRISTIAN PRAYER CENTER
http://www.christianprayercenter.com/
Contact form: http://www.christianprayercenter.com/

CHRISTIANS UNITED MINISTRIES, INC.
http://www.angelfire.com/al2/Pray/
http://www.christiansunitedministries.org/Home/Welcome.html
committed2prayer@hotmail.com
251-987-1234

CONSTANCE FREE CHURCH
http://www.constancefree.org/top_menu/prayer_requests
http://www.constancefree.org/
763-434-5995, ext. 29

CORNERSTONE TELEVISION
http://www.mycornerstone.tv/personalprayerrequests
http://www.ctvn.org/
888-665-4483

CROSSROADS
http://www.crossroads.ca/247care-online-prayer
http://www.crossroads.ca/247care
866-273-4444

DAYSTAR
http://www.daystar.com/prayer/submit-prayer-requests/
http://www.daystar.com/prayer/
English: 800-329-0029Spanish: 800-664-0029

DETROIT WORLD OUTREACH
http://www.dwo.org/contactus.php
http://www.dwo.org/
313-255-2222

DISCIPLESHIP EVANGELISM WORLDWIDE MINISTRY
http://www.dewwministry.org/
800-313-3399

DIVINE PRAYER LINE
http://www.divineprayerline.org/contact.htm
http://www.divineprayerline.org
divinefmprayer@yahoo.com
703-910-6646 or 703-910-6678

EVANGELICAL FREE CHURCH OF CANON CITY
http://www.efreechurch.org/
http://www.efreechurch.org/home
719-276-3007

PRAYER HOTLINES

FAITH PRAYERS
http://faithprayers.org/prayer/
http://faithprayers.org/
866-515-9406

FCCI—FELLOWSHIP OF COMPANIES FOR CHRIST INTERNATIONAL
http://www.fcci.org/prayer
http://www.fcci.org/
770-685-6000

FIRST BAPTIST CHURCH OF PICAYUNE
http://fbcpic.org/prayer-request/
http://fbcpic.org/
800-297-9462

FIRST UNITED METHODIST CHURCH
http://www.fcfumc.net/prayer-requests
http://www.fcfumc.net/index.php
970-482-2436, ext. 22

FOCUS ON THE FAMILY
http://www.focusonthefamily.com/
help@FocusontheFamily.com
800-232-6459

FREE CHAPEL
http://www.freechapel.org/prayer/

FREE-N-ONE
http://free-n-one.org/content/other-related-continuum-of-care/free-n-one-prayer-line/
http://www.free-n-one.org/content/
530-881-1000(Access Code: 688990#) Monday-Friday 6am (PST)
605-477-2100 (Access Code: 114851#) Monday-Friday 6am (PST)

GIVEN LIFE
http://www.givenlife.com/prayer/submit-your-prayer-request/
http://www.givenlife.com/

GLOBAL DESTINY PRAYER CENTER
http://www.iumi.org/index.php?p=1_36_TOLL-FREE-24-HOUR-CONFIDENTIAL-PRAYER-LINES
888-935-8100

GLOBAL PRAYER MINISTRIES
http://www.globalprayerministries.com/prayer_requests
http://www.globalprayerministries.com/
530-881-1400 PIN: 888974# or 712-432-0075 PIN: 607372#

GUIDEPOSTS
http://www.guideposts.org/ourprayer?int_source=front_page&int_medium=MainNavigation&int_campaign=SubmitaPrayer
http://www.guideposts.org/
800-204-3772

HOPE'S HOUSE
http://hopeshouse.com/new-here/need-prayer
http://hopeshouse.com/

ICC MINISTRIES (IMMACULATE CONCEPTION CHURCH)
http://icceaston.org/prayer-ministry
http://icceaston.org/
508-238-3195 or 508-238-3232

IMB CONNECTING
http://www.imb.org/main/contact.asp
800-999-3113 or 800-395-PRAY

INSIGHT FOR LIVING
http://www.insight.org/about/international/prayer.html
http://www.insight.org/
800-772-8888

THE SECRET PRAYER

JOEL OSTEEN
http://www.joelosteen.com/Pages/PrayTogether.aspx
http://www.joelosteen.com/Pages/Home.aspx
888-567-JOEL

JOHN HAGEE MINISTRIES
http://www.jhm.org/Resources/PrayerRequest
http://www.jhm.org/
210-491-5100

JOYCE MEYER
http://www.joycemeyer.org/EverydayAnswers/RequestPrayer.aspx
http://www.joycemeyer.org/home.aspx
800-727-9673 or for outside the US: 636-349-0303

KENNETH COPELAND MINISTRIES
http://www.kcm.org/forms/prayer
http://www.kcm.org/about/index.php?p=what_we_do
817-852-6000

KENNETH HAGIN
http://www.rhema.org/index.php?option=com_content&view=article&id=2006&Itemid=656
http://www.rhema.org/index.php?option=com_content&view=featured&Itemid=577
918-258-1588, ext. 5566

PRAYER HOTLINES

LAKEWOOD CHURCH
http://www.lakewoodchurch.com/Pages/Ministry.aspx?mid=1100
prayerrequest@lakewood.cc
713-491-1283

LESEA BROADCASTING
http://www.lesea.com/services/24-Hour-Prayerline.cfm
http://www.lesea.com/
800-365-3732 or 574-291-8200

LIFE TODAY
http://lifetoday.org/
feedback@lifetoday.org
800-947-5433

LIFESAVERS NATIONWIDE PRAYER MINISTRY
http://www.accesstogod.com/index.php/24-hour-toll-free-prayer-lines/
888-444-3458

LIVE PRAYER
http://www.liveprayer.com/
bkeller@liveprayer.com

THE SECRET PRAYER

LIVE PRAYER—ST. PETERSBURG, FL.
http://www.ibegin.com/directory/us/florida/st-petersburg/liveprayercom-6660-46th-ave-n/
727-546-9374

LOVE LINES, MN
612-379-1199

GRACE CHURCH LIFE—MCM PRAYER LINE
http://www.gracechurchlife.com/contacts/prayer_line.html
877-2-PRAY-NOW

MARILYN & SARAH—MARILYN HICKEY MINISTRIES
https://secure.marilynandsarah.org/contactus.aspx?&source=I14X-PRYX
http://www.marilynandsarah.org/
877-661-1249

MIKE SIMONS MINISTRIES
https://ww2.micahtek.com/nexolive/nPrayer.cfm?CFID=51439752&CFTOKEN=61722524
http://www.mikesimons.com/
800-717-0765

PRAYER HOTLINES

MORE THAN LIFE
http://www.morethanlife.org/prayer.
html?gclid=CPbx3bfNoMECFQsSMwodhAUAfA
E-mail: Enquiry@morethanlife.org or http://www.morethanlife.org/contact.html

MORRIS CERULLO HELP LINE
http://www.mcwe.com/ministry_details.php?id=5
http://www.mcwe.com/index.php
858-633-4885 or 858-277-2200

NEW DAY PRAYER MINISTRY
http://www.mynewday.tv/prayer-room
http://www.mynewday.tv/
800-665-5055

NEW LOTHROP
http://www.nlnaz.com/#/discover
http://www.nlnaz.com/#/home
877-638-5688

ORAL ROBERT'S PRAYER TOWER—TULSA, OK
http://www.roadsideamerica.com/story/2914
http://www.roadsideamerica.com/
918-495-6807 Tu-Sa 10am–3:30pm; Su 12:30–3:30pm

PENTECOSTAL MIRACLE MISSION
http://www.proudlyjesus.com/prayerline
http://www.proudlyjesus.com/contact
0800 911 777 (New Zealand)

PRAYER AND HOPE
http://www.prayerandhope.org/home.aspx
866-599-2264

PRAYER AND SPIRITUAL CARE
http://prayer.ag.org/
http://prayer.ag.org/about/
800-4-PRAYER (800-477-2937)

PRAYER IDEAS
info@prayerideas.org
http://www.prayerideas.org/

PRAYER PAGE
http://www.prayerpage.org/1800/prayer-lines.htm
800-4-PRAYER (800-477-2937) International: 44 1442-288-547

PRAY FOR ME
http://www.prayforme.com.au/uk-prayerline
http://www.prayforme.com.au/
0845 456 7729 (United Kingdom)

PRAYER HOTLINES

PULPIT CALLS
http://www.pulpitcalls.com/contact.php
http://www.pulpitcalls.com/

PUSH PRAYER MOVEMENT
http://www.pushprayer.org/prayer-request
http://www.pushprayer.org/

RHEMA MINISTRIES—TULSA, OK
http://www.rhemabiblechurch.com/
918-258-1588, ext. 2280

ROD PARSLEY'S BREAKTHROUGH MINISTRIES
http://orders.rodparsley.com/Order_First.aspx?ostr=PpHUQKkjgH4%3d
https://www.rodparsley.com/
866-241-4292

SALVATION ARMY PRAYER HOTLINE
http://www.salvationarmy.org/ihq/prayer
http://centralusa.salvationarmy.org/usc/submit_prayer_request
877-664-7729

THE SECRET PRAYER

SAY A PRAYER FOR MY PET
http://sayaprayerformypet.com/
http://sayaprayerformypet.com/index.php
949-800-5933

SILENT UNITY
http://www.unity.org/prayer
http://www.unity.org/
800-669-7729

SOMEBODY CARES—TAMPA BAY
http://www.sctb.org/prayerline.php
http://www.sctb.org/index.php
877-800-PRAY

TBN PRAYER AND PRAISE LINE
http://www.tbn.org/contact/prayer-request-form
http://www.tbn.org/
888-731-1000 or 714-832-2950

TD JAKES MINISTRIES
http://www.tdjakes.org/prayer/
http://www.tdjakes.org/
888-868-2497 or 800-BISHOP2

THERE IS HOPE
http://www.thereishoperadio.org/prayer.html
866-346-7186

PRAYER HOTLINES

THE UPPER ROOM
http://prayer-center.upperroom.org/
800-251-2468

THE VOICE FOR LOVE
http://www.thevoiceforlove.com/online-prayer-requests.html
http://www.thevoiceforlove.com/
http://www.thevoiceforlove.com/prayer-counseling-and-help-hotline.html
541-488-0426

TITUS HARVEST DOME SPECTRUM
http://www.rjwashington.org/prayer.html
http://www.rjwashington.org/aboutUs.html
888-TO-TITUS or 904-724-6769

TRUCKER OUT REACH—TRUCKERS FOR CHRIST (FOR TRUCKERS ONLY)
http://www.transportforchrist.org/contact/
http://www.transportforchrist.org/
800-632-8842

THE SECRET PRAYER

TRUCK STOP MINISTRIES (FOR TRUCKERS ONLY)
http://www.truckstopministry.com/
http://www.truckstopministry.com/HomePage-TruckStopMinistry.php
800-248-8662

UFBL—The Universal Foundation for Better Living, Inc.
http://ufbl.org/prayer/
877-375-8554

UMC Prayer Line (Christ United Methodist Church)
http://www.cumcsl.org/prayerandcare/prayer-request/
http://www.cumcsl.org/
281-980-6888, ext. 4779

UNITED METHODIST CHURCH GENERAL BOARD OF GLOBAL MINISTRIES
http://www.umcmission.org/
800-936-6893

UNITY OF AUSTIN
http://austinunity.moonfruit.com/#/daily-prayer-line/4570592112
info@unitychurchaustin.org
800-669-7729 or 512-892-3010 or Spanish: 816-969-2000

PRAYER HOTLINES

UPPER ROOM MINISTRIES—PRAYER CENTER
http://prayer-center.upperroom.org/request-prayer
http://prayer-center.upperroom.org/
800-251-2468 (7am–11pm CST)

VCY AMERICA (Christian Information Radio)
http://www.vcyamerica.org/prayerline.htm

VICTORY FOR THE WORLD
http://www.victoryfortheworld.org/contact-us.aspx
prayers@victoryfortheworld.org
678-476-6000

VICTORY OUTREACH INTERNATIONAL
http://victoryoutreach.org/connect/prayer-request/
909-599-4437

WHY PRAYER
http://www.whyprayer.com/contact-us/
http://www.whyprayer.com/

WORLD HARVEST PRAYERLINE
http://www.worldharvest.com/Share-a-prayer-need.cfm
http://www.worldharvest.com/
800-365-3732

WORLD MISSIONARY EVANGELISM
http://www.wme.org/prayerrequest.html
http://www.wme.org/
800-501-2851

WORLD NETWORK OF PRAYER
http://www.wnop.org/request-prayer-hp
http://www.wnop.org/
800-234-7729 or 214-837-7300

WORSHIP.NET
http://worship.net/
877-967-7447 or 800-477-2937 or 800-541-7729

WYBU TV16 (Your CTN Station Christian Television Network)
http://www.wybu.org/prayer-line.html
http://www.wybu.org/
800-716-7729 or 727-535-PRAY (7729)

ALL OTHER INTERNATIONAL CALLS
44 1442-288-547

BIBLIOGRAPHY

Allen, James. *As A Man Thinketh*. Lindenhurst, NY: Tribeca Books, 2011.

Audlin, Mindy. *What If It All Goes Right?* Garden City, NY: Morgan James, 2010.

Barton, Bruce. *What Can a Man Believe?* New York: Bobbs-Merrill, 1927.

Batterson, Mark. *The Grave Robber*. Grand Rapids: Baker Books, 2014.

Bowen, Will. *A Complaint-Free World*. New York: Harmony, 2013.

Breuning, Loretta. *Beyond Cynical*. San Francisco: Inner Mammal Institute, 2013.

———. *I, Mammal*. San Francisco: Inner Mammal Institute, 2011.

Davis, Bruce. *Monastery Without Walls: Daily Life in the Silence*. Lincoln, NE: iUniverse, 2001.

Dawson, W.J. *Prayer the Forgotten Secret*. New York: Revell, 1906.

Dickey, R.A. *Wherever I Wind Up: My Quest for Truth, Authenticity, and the Perfect Knuckleball*. New York: Blue Rider Press, 2012.

Dixon, Mathew. *Attracting for Others*. Wimberley, TX: Zero Limits, 2012.

Dossey, Larry. *Healing Words*. San Francisco: HarperOne, 1995.

Foulks, Frances W. *Effectual Prayer*. Life Summit, MO: Unity, 1964.

Fox, Emmet. *The Mental Equivalent*. Life Summit, MO: Unity, 1932.

———. *The Science of Living*. Farmingdale, NY: The Golden Keys, 2005.

Gaze, Harry. *Emmet Fox: The Man & His Work*. New York: Harper, 1952.

Goddard, Neville. *Neville Goddard Lecture Series*. 12 vols. Albuquerque: Audio Enlightenment Press, 2014.

Goddard, Neville. *The Neville Reader*. Camarillo, CA: DeVorss, 2005.

Helmer, George. *A Moment in Time: The Steve Reeves Story*. Mission Viejo, CA: Steve Reeves International, Inc., 2014.

Holmes, Ernest. *The Science of Mind*. New York: Tarcher, 2010.

Katie, Byron. *Loving What Is*. New York: Three Rivers Press, 2003.

Lawrence, Brother. *The Brother Lawrence Collection*. Radford, VA: Wilder Publications, 2008.

Levy, David. *Gray Matter: A Neurosurgeon Discovers the Power of Prayer…One Patient at a Time*. Carol Stream, IL: Tyndale House, 2011.

BIBLIOGRAPHY

Marden, Orison Swett. *He Can Who Thinks He Can.* New York: Crowell, 1927.

Metaxas, Eric. *Miracles.* New York: Dutton, 2014.

Moore, Tom. *The Gentle Way.* Flagstaff, AZ: Light Technology, 2006.

———. *The Gentle Way II.* Flagstaff, AZ: Light Technology, 2010.

Oden, Nerissa. *Bread-Free Bread.* Woodstock, VT: Countryman Press, 2014.

Orloff, Judith. *Second Sight.* New York: Harmony, 2010.

Parker, William, and Elaine St. Johns. *Prayer Can Change Your Life.* Carmel, NY: Guideposts, 1957.

Patterson, John Andrew. *An Answer for Every Prayer or The Mysteries of Prayer Revealed.* Holyoke, MA: Elizabeth Towne, 1926.

Ponder, Catherine. *The Dynamic Laws of Prayer.* Camarillo, CA: DeVorss, 1987. (Previously titled *Pray and Grow Rich.*)

Spilka, Bernard, and Kevin Ladd. *The Psychology of Prayer: A Scientific Approach.* New York: Guilford, 2013.

Teresa, Mother. *Where There Is Love, There Is God.* New York: Image Books, 2010.

Vitale, Joe. *Attract Money Now.* Wimberley, TX: Hypnotic Marketing, 2009.

———. *The Attractor Factor.* Hoboken, NJ: John Wiley & Sons, Inc., 2006.

———. *At Zero.* Hoboken, NJ: John Wiley & Sons, Inc., 2013.

———. *Faith.* Toronto: Burman Books, 2013.

———. *Life's Missing Instruction Manual.* Hoboken, NJ: John Wiley & Sons, Inc., 2006.

———. *Miracles Manual.* 2 vols. Wimberley, TX: Hypnotic Marketing. Accessed January 27, 2015. http://www.miraclesmanual.com.

———. *There's a Customer Born Every Minute.* Hoboken, NJ: John Wiley & Sons, Inc., 2006.

Vitale, Joe, and Daniel Barrett. *The Remembering Process.* San Diego: Hay House, 2014.

Vitale, Joe, and Dr. Ihaleakala Hew Len. *Zero Limits.* Hoboken, NJ: John Wiley & Sons, Inc., 2007.

Wattles, Wallace. *Financial Success Through Creative Thought* or *The Science of Getting Rich.* Holyoke, MA: Elizabeth Towne, 1915.

Discography

Vitale, Joe. *Afflatus.* Hypnotic Marketing, 2015, music album. http://www.AllHealingMusic.com

———. *Blue Healer.* Healing Mojo Music, 2011, music album.

———. *Healing Music.* Hypnotic Marketing, 2012, music album.

———. *Reflection.* Hypnotic Marketing, 2014, music album. http://www.ReflectionCD.com

ABOUT THE AUTHOR

Dr. Joe Vitale—once homeless but now a motivating *inspirator* known to his millions of fans as "Mr. Fire!"—is the globally famous author of numerous best-selling books, such as *The Attractor Factor*, *Zero Limits*, *Life's Missing Instruction Manual,* and *Attract Money Now* (free at www.AttractMoneyNow.com).

He is a star in the blockbuster movie *The Secret,* as well as a dozen other films. He has recorded many best-selling audio programs, from *The Missing Secret* to *The Zero Point*. He's also the world's first self-help singer-songwriter, with fifteen albums released and many of his songs nominated for the Posi Award (considered the Grammy's of positive music).

He created Miracles Coaching®, The Awakening Course, The Secret Mirror, The Secret Reflection, and many more life transforming products. He lives outside of Austin, Texas with his wife, Nerissa, and their pets.

See www.JoeVitale.com

FOLLOW DR. JOE VITALE

Twitter: https://twitter.com/mrfire
Facebook: https://www.facebook.com/drjoevitale
Blog: http://blog.mrfire.com/

Get *Attract Money Now!*
by Dr. Joe Vitale

FREE!

ATTRACT MONEY NOW

EASY 7-STEP FORMULA

DR. JOE VITALE
AUTHOR OF *ZERO LIMITS* AND *THE ATTRACTOR FACTOR*

From the Author of the bestselling book

ATTRACTOR FACTOR — JOE VITALE

The ATTRACTOR FACTOR

and featured in *The Secret*

and on **Larry King LIVE** (twice)

Read for FREE at
www.AttractMoneyNow.com

WHEN YOU LOOK IN YOUR MIRROR, WHAT DO YOU HEAR?

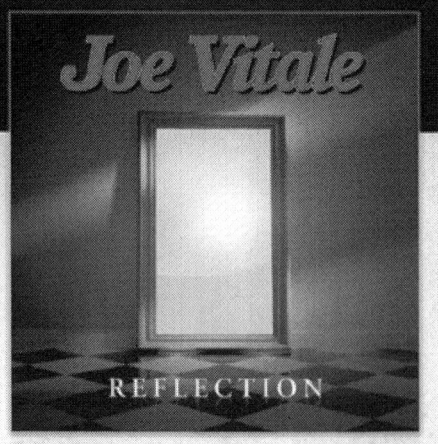

Joe Vitale

REFLECTION

Hear www.ReflectionCD.com

BLUE HEALER	**STRUT!**	**ALIGNING TO ZERO**	**THE HEALING SONG**	**AT ZERO**	**SUN WILL RISE**
HealingMojoMusic.com	GetUpAndStrut.com	AligningToZero.info	TheHealingSong.com	AtZeroMusic.com	HealingRockMusic.com

Dr. Joe Vitale is a bestselling author, musician, movie star, marketer, Law of Attraction expert, and more. Creator of Miracles Coaching® and The Secret Mirror™. Star in the hit movie "The Secret."
See www.JoeVitale.com

SPECIAL MIRACLES COACHING® OFFER!

For the past 25 years I've been helping people like you attract ALL kinds of miracles in EVERY area of their lives.

I've helped people attract...
**Money • Cars • Soul Mates • Better Health
New Careers • Dream Homes**

The list goes on and on! And I can help you do the same in my *Joe Vitale's Miracles Coaching® Program*! The key is for you to be ready. (And it looks like you are or you would not be reading this right now). If you want to learn more about how you can attract money, jobs, health, love, careers, relationships or anything else quickly, and you want to sign up now, just go to...

www.miraclescoaching.com

Made in the USA
Lexington, KY
26 May 2016